THE POWER IN DIGITAL PERFORMER

quick **PRO**
guides

THE POWER IN DIGITAL PERFORMER

David E. Roberts

Hal Leonard Books
An Imprint of Hal Leonard Corporation

Published in 2012 by Hal Leonard Books
An Imprint of Hal Leonard Corporation
7777 West Bluemound Road
Milwaukee, WI 53213

Trade Book Division Editorial Offices
33 Plymouth St., Montclair, NJ 07042

Printed in the United States of America

Book design by Adam Fulrath
Book composition by Kristina Rolander

Library of Congress Cataloging-in-Publication Data is available upon request.

ISBN 978-1-4768-1514-5

www.halleonardbooks.com

CONTENTS

Chapter 3

Chapter 4

Chapter 5

Chapter 10

THE POWER IN DIGITAL PERFORMER

quick**PRO**
guides

INTRODUCTION

Digital Performer is digital audio workstation software for a Mac or Windows computer. It is a powerful tool used for music composition and production, as well as many other related functions. This book is a practical introduction to Digital Performer.

In this text I will describe step-by-step how to design, set up, and customize a system to your own requirements. When we're through, you will have a solid understanding of how to record, edit, and mix your music. Along the way we will discuss virtual instruments, mastering, scoring music for video, and other key aspects of using Digital Performer.

Digital Performer, version 8 (DP8), works the same way on a Mac or Windows computer. The information in this book applies to both platforms.

The first portion of this book is a methodical description of how to use the basic functions of the software. Reading through these chapters will provide a solid foundation for understanding and becoming an expert with Digital Performer. The book's last chapter is devoted to a step-by-step procedure for building a musical composition from start to finish, allowing the reader to immediately start making music and exploring the program.

Each chapter is self-contained. For example, if Digital Performer is already installed and running on your computer, skip the chapters on requirements and setup, and go straight to the chapters on specific functions within the software.

The Power in Digital Performer is designed to be task oriented. It is not simply a list of every button and menu choice in Digital Performer. It is my goal to provide the basic information needed in order to start making music as quickly as possible. This book is written to be a companion to the Digital Performer manual, which is an encyclopedia of all the functions in the software. If further detail on any function mentioned in this book is required, check the index of the Digital Performer manual and you will very likely find that additional information.

We will start from the beginning and before you know it, you will be a Digital Performer Power User!

The Included DVD

The DVD included with this book contains movie files and a Digital Performer project. The movies provide examples of specific functions within Digital Performer, and show how to create and complete a song in Digital Performer, from start to finish.

There is a Digital Performer demo project on the DVD that is a finished composition. The project makes use of MIDI tracks, audio tracks, virtual instruments, and effects plug-ins. To use this file, it must first be copied to the computer's hard drive. Digital Performer, version 8, must be installed on your computer. The Digital Performer session file can then be opened and explored. The demo project is described in detail in the appendix.

A General Description of Digital Performer

Digital Performer provides many different creative tools and options. The list of features is comprehensive.

- It is software that turns a computer into a digital audio workstation (DAW).
- It records, edits, and plays audio and MIDI.
- It hosts virtual software instruments.
- It provides part and score notation features for sheet music and lead sheets. Professional-quality sheet music can be printed from any printer or saved as a PDF or graphics file.
- It plays back digital video files and is a powerful tool for creating soundtracks for movies.
- It includes all the tools required to do multichannel surround sound production.
- It can be used in live performance for signal processing, recording, and playback. In a large stage production, Digital Performer can play back audio, MIDI, and video, as well as generate time code that is used to run lights, pyrotechnics, and mechanized staging. Digital Performer can run the entire show.

Digital Performer can do many things and is a very powerful tool, both in the studio and onstage. It contains everything you need to work, from the initial creative idea to the final mastered project.

Digital Performer is also designed to be as obvious how to use as possible. The simplest task can be easy to do—if you know the basics. Let's get started!

Chapter 1
SETTING UP THE STUDIO

Digital Performer, version 8, can run on an Apple computer or on a PC that is running Windows. There are minimum computer requirements to run Digital Performer. This chapter will describe the specific computer requirements necessary to run a stable and efficient Digital Performer system.

Besides a compatible computer, no other software or external hardware is required to install and run Digital Performer. However, there are many ways to expand a Digital Performer system. This chapter will discuss what basic peripheral hardware is used with Digital Performer and how to expand a system for specific studio requirements.

Computer Requirements

In order to run any software program, a computer must meet the minimum specified requirements of that software. A current top-of-the-line Mac or Windows computer far exceeds the minimum requirements needed to run Digital Performer. To run any computer with maximum efficiency, it is useful to understand how the specifications of the computer will affect performance of Digital Performer.

Commercial software companies such as MOTU develop their software and hardware products on stock computers and operating systems. If the computer has to be customized to run the software, the developer would have to tell potential customers that fact ahead of time. Digital Performer is designed to run on a stock computer running a standard Mac or Windows operating system.

There are minimum specifications that the computer must have for the software to run properly. In the case of a real-time program such as Digital Performer, the relative power of the computer can make a difference to the performance of the software. What this means is that if the computer is at the minimum specification to run Digital Performer, it will not be able to give the same level of performance as a more powerful system. That isn't a problem as long as there is a reasonable understanding and expectation of what a specific system is capable of doing. A more powerful computer will allow Digital Performer to record and play more audio tracks and apply more effects to those tracks. A more powerful computer can make a significant difference in terms of how many simultaneous virtual instruments can be run.

When looking at the specifications of your computer, there are basic considerations that are common to both Mac and Windows. These specifications make the difference between having a minimum system or a system with maximum capability.

I currently am using an Apple MacBook Pro with a 3.06 GHz Intel Core Duo 2 CPU. It has 8 GB of RAM and a 500 GB SSD hard drive. This computer can easily play back 48 tracks of audio with full effects for a complete mixdown. It's also used onstage to run Digital Performer for live guitar processing and virtual instrument triggering. As of this writing this is a two-year-old computer, and it is more than powerful enough for professional requirements.

Operating System (OS)

An operating system is the software that launches when a computer first boots up. Digital Performer runs inside the OS. Digital Performer, version 8, can run on Mac OS X 10.6 or higher, and on the 32- or 64-bit editions of Windows 7.

CPU Type and Speed

Digital Performer requires an Intel-based Apple computer or a current generation Intel Pentium or an Advanced Micro Devices–based Windows computer. MOTU recommends a minimum CPU speed of 1 GHz. Any current Apple or Windows computer will exceed that minimum specification.

Digital Performer can take full advantage of multiple processors and hyperthreading. More CPU power means more audio tracks, more real-time effects, and more virtual instruments.

When buying a computer, there is always a certain aspect of "you get what you pay for" involved. If the computer is underpowered, it may be unstable and prone to crashes. Working with an underpowered computer can be a frustrating experience. Conversely, if a computer is more powerful than what is needed, money is being wasted on the extra horsepower that is not being used.

Reasonable general advice is that a top-of-the-line computer system is justified if all that power is needed to get the specific job done. For example, a person who composes music for movies may need to run an orchestra's worth of virtual instruments, as well as literally hundreds of audio and MIDI tracks, while also playing back large video files. This situation can justify a top-of-the-line multiprocessor computer loaded with RAM and extra drives. For a more modest system, a less powerful computer will do just as good a job as the more powerful and more expensive machine.

RAM

RAM is used by a computer CPU to store instructions and data. When a program such as Digital Performer is launched, its software code is called up from the hard drive into the computer RAM.

A great deal of what Digital Performer can do is in *real time*, which means an external controller such as a MIDI keyboard or drum pads can be used to trigger and play virtual instruments within Digital Performer. Live signals, such as a guitar or a voice, can be routed through Digital Performer for processing onstage or in the studio. Effects can be added to audio tracks, and changes made to those effects will be heard in real time. This type of work requires a computer that has a powerful CPU and a substantial amount of RAM.

The absolute minimum amount of RAM to launch and run Digital Performer is 2 GB. With that minimum amount of RAM, the program will not be able to get a great deal of real-time performance. With the minimum amount of RAM, Digital Performer will do basic MIDI sequencing and recording or playback of a few audio tracks.

The recommended minimum amount of RAM to run Digital Performer is 4 GB. This will at least provide stable performance and the ability to run virtual instruments.

More than 4 GB RAM will allow Digital Performer to run much larger projects, with more audio tracks, effects, and in particular, virtual instruments. Sample-based virtual instruments use the most memory of any task in a DAW. For a large multiprocessor computer, the primary benefit of adding larger amounts of RAM is that Digital Performer will be able to run more simultaneous virtual instruments.

DP8 can run as a 32- or 64-bit application under the Mac or Windows OS. Running in 32-bit mode means that Digital Performer is restricted to accessing no more than 4 GB of RAM. Very simply, running in 64-bit mode means that Digital Performer is not restricted to 4 GB of RAM; running in 64-bit means that Digital Performer can host very large sample-based virtual instruments, and those instruments can access as much RAM as is available within the computer. By default, DP8 is set to run as a 64-bit application on a Mac computer. On a Windows 7 computer, DP8 runs in 32- or 64-bit mode based on the mode of the OS.

Hard Drives

Digital Performer installs from a DVD.

You can also use a DVD read/write drive to efficiently archive large project files.

Digital Performer gets installed onto the system drive of the computer. The stock internal drive of the computer can be used to run the entire DAW system.

On my own laptop computer, the internal drive is used for all tasks. In addition to the OS and Digital Performer, there is also a library of samples for virtual instruments. Video is played back from the internal drive. Audio is recorded and played back from the internal drive.

Having said that, the type and speed of the drive does make a difference to overall performance. Also, different tasks use the hard drive in different ways. Therefore, a top-of-the-line optimized system may use multiple drives for different tasks.

Hard drives may be spinning disks, or they may be solid-state devices. A solid-state drive is more expensive, but faster. If the drive is a spinning disk, it may be a 5,400 rpm, 7,200 rpm, 9,600 rpm, or faster drive. The faster the drive, the better the performance. A RAID (redundant array of independent disks) drive setup is not required and most likely will not increase performance.

Drives can connect to the computer in several different ways. The connection type will also have an impact on performance. An internal drive connected directly to the CPU will be the most efficient connection. Drives can also connect via FireWire, USB, or eSATA connection. A new connection technology called Thunderbolt is currently being developed, and that will also be a very efficient way to connect hard drives.

Reasonable advice to a new Digital Performer user is to start with the stock internal drive of the computer. On a current-generation Mac or Windows computer, the stock internal drive should be at least powerful enough to play back 24 tracks of audio.

Even if the internal drive of the computer is fast enough to do all the work required, there is still the question of file storage. Digital audio files are large and therefore require some sort of backup plan. Sample-based virtual instrument libraries can take up large amounts of drive space, and therefore it may be useful to have a hard drive dedicated to virtual instrument sample libraries.

Here is a list of basic audio file sizes:

- 16-bit, 44.1 kHz audio (CD standard format) uses about 5 MB of drive space for each mono minute of audio
- 24-bit, 44.1 kHz audio uses about 7 MB per mono track minute
- 24-bit, 96 kHz audio uses roughly 14 MB per mono track minute

Therefore, a three-minute project with 24 tracks of 24-bit, 44.1 kHz audio will use just over 500 MB of disk space to store the audio.

The old computer wisdom is that if critical data is backed up, the data will never be lost. There is also an inverse law that says if the data is not backed up, it will eventually be lost. The question is, "What will that mean if the data is lost?" If it's a quick scratch idea, perhaps the idea can be remembered and recorded again. If the data represents the past six months of work on a project that was going to pay the rent, that is a bigger problem. Therefore, back up all critical data!

A few last words on hard drives: A great deal of data gets written to a hard drive, and that data gets moved around constantly. If something happens to corrupt the data on the hard drive, there will be problems that could result in the total loss of all data on the drive. This type of technical computer problem has nothing to do with being creative, and can be a real inspiration-killer. It's a good idea to be in the habit of being organized with your data on the hard drives. Don't copy random files to random locations. When a new Digital Performer project is created, be aware of where that project is created.

Keep all hard drives in good working order. Never fill a drive to capacity. Always try to have at least 3 to 5 GB of empty space on the drive. It is a good idea to run drive maintenance utilities from time to time.

Video Monitors

When we talk about a computer, it's assumed that the computer also includes a keyboard, mouse, and monitor screen. Although Digital Performer can run on a very small monitor, it's much easier on the eyes to have plenty of screen "real estate" for doing detailed work. When using Digital Performer for live performance (playback, signal processing, and virtual instrument hosting), a large monitor is not required for those jobs. In the studio, a second or third monitor may be a useful addition.

The interface of Digital Performer is highly customizable, and it's possible to place different Digital Performer windows on different monitors. A typical setup could be to place the mixing board on one monitor and an editing window on a second monitor. If Digital Performer is also playing back video, an additional monitor just for the Movie window may be desirable.

Depending on the physical capabilities of the computer, it may be possible to connect multiple monitor screens. Using multiple monitors is a personal preference. It's not a requirement. Having said that, working with a DAW system equipped with two or three large monitors can be a real pleasure.

A Sample Configuration

For the sake of perspective, I will describe the computer that I use for my own work. I do multitrack recording in the studio and use the computer in live performance to host virtual instruments and process live guitar signals.

My recording system is based around a laptop computer. There is a secondary hard drive that is used for temporary backup and the bulk of my sample library. All work is done on the internal drive of the computer. Project files are copied to the backup drive at the end of each work session so that there is more than one copy of the project. When the project is completed, all data is backed up by archiving to DVDs.

On the internal drive of my computer is the basic instrument library. The complete sample library is stored on an external drive.

Conclusion

A factory stock, current-generation Apple or Windows computer with 4 to 8 GB of installed RAM will provide you with a solid platform to get started with Digital Performer. To increase performance, more RAM and hard drives can be added as required.

Studio Requirements

Besides the computer and recording software, there are a few other basic hardware requirements for setting up a digital audio workstation. The following section will describe the basic requirements for a complete system

Speakers and Headphones

A music-production system requires a way to monitor audio signals. Speakers and headphones are used for this job. Most computers have built-in speakers and headphone outputs. If the computer has built-in audio inputs and outputs, Digital Performer can use those connections. In some cases, this may be all that is required in order to do work. For better-quality playback, external speakers can be used. A good set of monitor speakers or high-quality headphones are never a bad investment.

The quality of the built-in audio outputs of most computers is usually good enough to do basic composition, editing, and mixing work. One way to judge the quality of the built-in audio outputs is to listen to a commercial CD played back from the computer.

External speakers can be connected to the built-in audio outputs of the computer. For a more sophisticated system, a separate audio interface is used to provide high-quality audio inputs and outputs to the computer. The audio interface connects to the computer, typically with USB, FireWire, or similar type of connector. Speakers and headphones connect to the audio outputs of the audio interface.

Digital Performer generates sound when it plays back audio files or movies with audio tracks. If Digital Performer is used to host virtual instruments, those instruments generate audio signals. It's also possible to use Digital Performer for live processing of an external audio signal. For example, a guitar can be patched into the computer, through Digital Performer, and out to speakers or headphones. The guitar signal can be processed in real time by Digital Performer with effects plug-ins that emulate guitar amplifiers, speaker cabinets, and effects. This means that Digital Performer can be used to process audio in a live performance setting. For the job of live processing of external audio, the computer needs both audio output and input capabilities.

It is conceivable that Digital Performer may be used in a way that doesn't require audio output at all. For example, if Digital Performer is being used to work with music notation, audio output is not required for note entry, editing, or printing.

Microphones

Microphones are used to record acoustic sounds such as voice or acoustic guitar. The sonic qualities of the microphone have a direct bearing on the quality of the recording. Different microphones have different sonic characteristics. A well-equipped recording studio usually has a collection of different types of microphones. There are several different categories of microphones. Understanding the differences between microphones enables a recording engineer to pick the best microphone for the job.

Condenser microphones are a typical choice for studio recording. A good condenser microphone is an excellent starting point for a recording studio. Condenser microphones usually have a wide dynamic range and wide frequency response.

Condenser microphones may have a wide range of pickup patterns, which can help give a natural ambient sound. Condenser microphones require external power, which is usually supplied from a preamp that generates phantom power. Some condenser microphones have dedicated external power supplies. Some condenser microphones can be powered via an internal battery.

Microphones that are used onstage for live sound reinforcement are generally dynamic microphones. Dynamic mics are generally rugged and can take the abuse of being used onstage. A dynamic microphone does not require a power source. Dynamic microphones sometime have a narrow pickup pattern and frequency response that's less responsive in the low frequencies and often more responsive in a specific high-frequency range. This makes them a good choice for close-miking an instrument or voice because moving the mic closer to the source causes an increase in low frequencies. Also, the extra sensitivity in the high frequencies adds clarity to the sound. Dynamic microphones typically can accept very loud input signals. Dynamic microphones can certainly be used for recording. A typical use of a dynamic microphone in a recording studio is for a snare drum or guitar amplifier.

A third category is the ribbon microphone. Ribbon microphones are similar to dynamic microphones in that they do not require external power. Ribbon microphones have bidirectional pickup patterns. Ribbon microphones typically have a high-frequency roll-off and relatively low signal output. Ribbon microphones can be used for voice, and are commonly used to record guitar amplifiers.

Any microphone can be used for recording. Very cheap microphones will generally have a poor quality of sound. However, for less than $200, there are many high-quality microphones available. If possible, visit a music store or pro audio dealer and spend some time comparing the sound of different microphones.

Audio Interfaces

An audio interface is a piece of hardware that connects to the computer in order to provide high-quality audio inputs and outputs. Such a device can be a little box that sits on the desktop, or it can be an array of rackmounted hardware for a larger system. Some models of audio interfaces also include direct input to output monitoring capabilities. This will be discussed in detail in the section on audio monitoring. An audio interface may also include additional signal processing functions such as EQ, dynamics, reverb, or other effects.

A dedicated audio interface has several advantages over the built-in sound card of the computer. The sonic quality of a dedicated audio interface is typically better than the quality of a built-in sound card. When recording audio into a computer, the quality of the analog-to-digital converter has a direct bearing on the audio quality of the final project.

Digital Performer supports standard audio driver protocols on Mac and Windows . On Mac, the Apple Core Audio standard is supported. On Windows, WDM (Microsoft) and ASIO drivers are supported. This means that if the audio interface works with the computer and uses one of these driver types, it will be compatible with Digital Performer.

There are many available audio interfaces made by many different companies. To choose the appropriate model of audio interface, answer the questions on this checklist: How many channels of input and output are required? What formats of inputs and outputs are required? How will the interface connect to the computer? Does the interface need to be expandable? Are additional features such as MIDI input and output ports, internal mixers, and internal effects processing required? Once these specifications are worked out, it is much simpler to select a model of audio interface that meets these requirements.

In order to record a stereo audio signal, two channels of audio input are required. To record four tracks of audio at the same time, four separate channels of input are required. The built-in sound card on the computer may be adequate for two channels of input. To do more than two tracks of recording at a time, an external audio interface will be required. The number of audio tracks that can be recorded in a single pass is limited by the number of actual inputs on the audio interface.

It's important to understand the difference between channels and tracks in this context. Channels are physical paths in and out of the computer. Tracks record and play back within the computer. To record eight simultaneous, separate tracks of audio, eight separate channels of input are required. To play back a stereo mix of those eight separate tracks, only two channels of output are required.

To play back a stereo mix from the computer, two channels of audio output are required for monitoring. To play back a 5.1 surround mix, six separate channels of output are required.

To create separate monitor mixes for different musicians, separate outputs for each of those mixes are required.

It is possible to patch external audio processing gear into a computer-based mixdown. Separate audio inputs and outputs are required for each of those external devices.

If an external mixer is used for multitrack mixdown from Digital Performer, separate audio outputs are required for each track that is to be sent to that external mixer.

There are different formats of audio connections that may be found on an audio interface. A microphone or guitar generates a very weak signal and typically needs to be plugged into a preamplifier input. A synthesizer, mixer, or external preamplifier will generate a stronger audio signal that connects to a line level input. It is also be possible to connect external devices to an audio interface with digital audio cables. Examples of digital audio format connections include S/PDIF, TDIF, ADAT, AES/EBU, TOSLink, and others.

Audio interfaces can connect to the computer via PCI card, ExpressCard, FireWire, or USB. A new technology called Thunderbolt is being developed for Mac and Windows computers, and there will be audio interfaces that use this protocol. The type of connection between the audio interface and computer is significant, because different types of connections can pass different amounts of data. The amount of data that can pass translates into the number of channels used. The greater the bandwidth, the larger the number of channels that can pass. For example, USB and FireWire connections cannot pass as many channels of audio as can PCI or Thunderbolt. Because higher sample rates mean larger amounts of data, sample rate also has a bearing on how many channels of audio can pass over a specific connection.

USB and FireWire can pass at least 24 channels of audio. That means that if a system needs to be able to record 24 channels of simultaneous audio, a FireWire or USB interface may be just as functional as a PCI- or Thunderbolt-based interface. As a general rule, if a system needs to have 32 or more channels of audio input or output, a PCI or Thunderbolt connection will be required.

Any device that connects to a computer requires a software driver in order for the computer to recognize and work with that device. The Mac and Windows operating systems have some basic device drivers already built in. For some simple audio interfaces, all that is required is to connect to the computer and the computer will automatically recognize and work with that device. For more sophisticated audio interfaces, separate drivers may need to be installed in order for the computer to work with that hardware.

MIDI Interfaces, Controllers, and Sound Modules

A MIDI controller is a physical device that is used to generate MIDI messages. Examples of MIDI controllers include keyboards, drum trigger pads, guitar-to-MIDI converters, as well as devices such as footpedals or dedicated control surfaces. The MIDI controller generates MIDI and sends that signal into the computer to Digital Performer. To trigger sound, MIDI is then passed to a virtual instrument, or out to an external sound module.

Some MIDI controllers have their own built-in MIDI interface, and provide a USB port to connect directly to the computer. As with any device that connects to the computer, a software driver is required for the device to be recognized. Some USB controllers may be automatically recognized by the computer. Other devices may require that specific software drivers be installed. Mac and Windows systems use standard driver protocols for MIDI I/O. If the MIDI device works with Apple Core MIDI protocol, or with Microsoft WDM protocol, it will work with Digital Performer.

If the goal is to trigger sound from a MIDI controller, that sound needs to be generated somehow. MIDI-triggered sound is typically generated by a synthesizer or a sampler (or possibly a hybrid of both). Synthesizers and samplers can be hardware devices. Synthesizers and samplers can also exist as software devices called *virtual instruments*.

To trigger virtual instruments with an external MIDI controller, there must be a way to get the MIDI signal from the controller into the computer. If the MIDI controller has a built-in USB connection, and all the sound sources are virtual instruments, the setup is very simple. Use a USB cable to connect the controller to the computer, and that is all the external MIDI connection that is required.

If external sound modules are used, there needs to be a way to get MIDI from the computer out to those modules. If the USB-equipped MIDI controller also has the capability to be a sound module, the single USB connection may be all that is required. For additional MIDI devices that don't have USB connections, a dedicated MIDI interface can be used to provide those additional inputs and outputs.

A MIDI interface is a hardware device that provides MIDI inputs and outputs and connects to the computer, usually with a USB cable. If there are MIDI devices that don't have USB connections, or if there are multiple MIDI devices that need to be connected to the computer, that's the time to get a MIDI interface. Depending on the model, a MIDI interface may have one to eight or more MIDI input and output ports. If there are multiple MIDI devices to be connected, the proper solution is to get a MIDI interface that has enough ports to accommodate each piece of gear. Dedicated MIDI interfaces may have one to eight MIDI input and output ports, depending on the model. Some models of audio interfaces also feature MIDI input and output ports.

Mixers and Other Hardware Processors

An external mixer is not required to use Digital Performer. However, an external mixer may be a useful addition to a recording studio, depending on the requirements and preferences of the person operating the system.

In a recording studio, a hardware mixer has three general roles. A mixer can be used as an input point for audio signals. Microphones, keyboards, and other audio signals can be patched into a hardware mixing board. The mixer may provide functions such as phantom power and preamps for microphones. A common use of a mixer is to submix multiple signals together. For example, a group of synthesizers can be mixed to a stereo submix, and then sent into the computer to be recorded as a single stereo track.

An external mixer can be used as a monitor station. External audio signals and playback from the computer can be routed through the mixer to headphones and speakers.

An external mixer can be used to mix down multiple tracks of playback from the computer. To do this, an audio interface with enough output channels to pass the separate tracks from the computer to the mixer is also required.

All of the functions of an external mixer can be duplicated with an audio interface and the functions inside Digital Performer. Whether you use an external mixing board is based purely on personal preference.

It is possible to use external processing devices when recording or mixing with Digital Performer. Some audio engineers have favorite hardware processors that they like to use in a computer-based recording session.

An external processor can be used in line to process a signal before it is recorded. An example of this is when a guitar player uses effects pedals when playing live. Another example is when you patch a vocal microphone through hardware processors such as vacuum tube preamps, EQs, compressors, de-essers, and so on.

External processing hardware can be used in a computer-based mixdown. For example, the final stereo mix from the computer could be run through external processing gear and then routed back into the computer to be recorded as a final stereo mix. External effects processors can be used with sends and returns for individual tracks within a Digital Performer mix.

Control Surfaces

Digital Performer can be controlled in different ways. Because Digital Performer is software, you have the usual computer controls of mouse and keyboard. You can control Digital Performer from an external device such as a simple MIDI controller. More sophisticated external control can be achieved via an iPad, an iPhone, or a similar tablet device. There are also dedicated hardware devices that can be used to control Digital Performer.

MIDI hardware controllers can be used to send command messages to Digital Performer. Digital Performer can be controlled by assigned keys on a MIDI keyboard, MIDI drum trigger pads, MIDI footswitch controllers, or any device that generates MIDI notes, controller commands, or patch change messages. The external device sends MIDI messages into Digital Performer, and Digital Performer responds to those messages. This is set up in the Commands window under the Setup menu. Fader and panner assignment is configured from the Digital Performer mixing board minimenu. The limitation of simple external MIDI control is that it is a one-way communication. If an external slider is mapped to a fader on the Digital Performer mixing board, moving that external fader will move the fader in Digital Performer. However, moving the fader on the Digital Performer mixing board will not send a message back to move the slider on the external controller.

Digital Performer can be controlled by external software and hardware that communicates bidirectionally. The control surface sends commands to Digital Performer, and Digital Performer send commands and other information back to the control surface. This means that if a fader is moved in the Digital Performer Mixing Board window, the corresponding fader on the control surface moves in response.

There are several different protocols for bidirectional control surface support in Digital Performer. Mackie has implemented HUI and Mackie Universal Control support. Devices that support these protocols can be used to control Digital Performer. Digital Performer is supported by the Eucon protocol from Avid Technology for its MC Mix and MC Control devices. Digital Performer can be controlled via a software protocol called OSC (Open Sound Control). OSC allows software running on a device such as an iPad to control Digital Performer over a computer network. Digital Performer can also be controlled from an iPad, iPod Touch, or iPhone

Figure 1.1

with the DP Control app, which can be downloaded for free from the Apple App Store. (To download the DP Control app, go to http://itunes.apple.com/ie/app/dp-control/id380483770?mt=8.)

Bidirectional control surfaces are configured in Digital Performer via the Control Surface Setup under the Setup menu. Press the Add button to create a control surface driver. Follow the instructions that came with the specific control surface to configure the device in Digital Performer.

Audio Monitoring

Audio monitoring is simply listening to the sound that is being recorded or played back. An audio monitoring system consists of speakers and/or headphones, and a routing system to get signals to those speakers and phones. In a recording system, the musicians and recording engineer have to be able to hear the live instruments, as well as the playback of previously recorded instruments. The audio monitoring system provides this capability.

Perhaps the most critical components of a music production system are the monitor speakers or headphones. In order to make music, the music that comes from those pieces must be audible. A fully equipped recording studio may have multiple speakers systems, as well as an array of headphones. A simple DAW setup may rely on a small set of speakers and a single set of headphones.

If external sound modules are used in the DAW system, there needs to be a way to monitor those audio signals. If audio is to be recorded, there needs to be a way to monitor that signal as it is being recorded. For example, if a singer is wearing a pair of headphones and says "testing" into a microphone, the singer needs be able to hear his or her voice in the headphones. That means there needs to be an audio path not just from the computer to the speakers or headphones, but also from external sound sources all the way through to the audio monitors.

Ideally, a recording system should be ready to go when it is powered on. If no sound comes out of the audio monitors, there is a problem. It's very difficult to be creative while also trying to troubleshoot a system. At the very least, having an awareness of the signal path from the external sound sources, and from the computer to the audio monitors, is a good thing to master. This concept of signal flow will be mentioned many times in this book. Where does a signal originate? How does it get from one place to another? How does that signal ultimately get to the audio monitors?

There are many ways to set up a recording system. There are conventions and typical designs that audio engineers use. However, there really are no rules. If the system works and is comfortable to use, that is the bottom line.

The DAW system may be very simple. For example, the setup could consist of a laptop computer with a set of headphones and an external USB MIDI controller keyboard.

Figure 1.2

In this example, MIDI is generated by the controller keyboard and sent into the computer via USB. Sound is generated inside the computer by virtual instrument software, and is sent to the computer speakers or headphones.

Two Ways to Monitor Input Signals

With a computer-based DAW system, there are two fundamental ways to monitor an audio signal from input to output. An external audio signal can be patched into the computer, through Digital Performer, and out of the computer to the audio monitors. The second method for monitoring is to use a separate mixer to route the input signal directly to the audio monitors, without being patched through the computer. Both of these methods are commonly used.

Direct monitoring is when an audio signal is patched directly from input to output. This can be done with an external mixer. Some audio interfaces have built-in mixers. The disadvantage of direct monitoring is that the live signal is not being monitored through Digital Performer, and therefore the signal cannot be monitored through effects plug-ins. The advantage of direct monitoring is that there is no load on the computer for the live processing, and no latency delay in the monitored signal.

When an audio interface provides direct monitoring functions, it is doing two jobs. When the external audio signal is connected to the input of the interface, the signal is sent to the computer for recording or live processing. The signal is also sent to the internal mixer of the audio interface. The mixer in the audio interface is typically controlled from its front panel or from some sort of control software inside the computer. Some audio interface mixers can also be controlled directly from Digital Performer. This will be discussed in the section "Audio Input Monitoring" in chapter 2, "Installation and Getting Started," which is on running Digital Performer for the first time.

Monitoring audio through Digital Performer allows the signal to be processed though plug-in effects in real time. For example, a vocal microphone can be patched through Digital Performer, and delay or reverb can be added to the monitored signal as the singer is laying down his or her track. Because the effects are on the output of the monitored signal, they are not printed to the audio file and can be changed at any time during mixdown.

Another example of monitoring through Digital Performer is for live performance. Digital Performer can function as a host for real-time processing of live audio signals. For example, a guitar can be routed through Digital Performer to be processed with amp and speaker cabinet simulation, as well as any other effects the guitarist would like to use onstage. The processed signal is then sent directly to the PA system. This means no more carrying around amplifiers and pedalboards!

A signal should be monitored through only one path. If the signal is monitored directly through the audio interface or an external mixer, it should not simultaneously be monitored through Digital Performer. If the audio input signal is "double-monitored." there will be two problems. The signals will combine to have phase cancellation, which will sound very bad. Also, having a doubled monitor path means that there is no single point at which the monitor volume of that signal can be controlled.

It is not unusual to use a combination of direct monitoring, as well as monitoring through Digital Performer. For example, external sound modules may be patched directly through the audio interface while a vocal microphone and guitar signals are being processed through Digital Performer.

An Example of a Monitoring Setup

The example below shows a microphone plugged into the input of an audio interface. The audio interface is connected to the computer via USB or FireWire. The headphones or monitor speakers are connected to the outputs of the audio interface.

Figure 1.3

There are two possible paths for the microphone signal to reach the headphones. The microphone signal can be passed into and through Digital Performer and back out to the headphones.

Figure 1.4

Because this model of audio interface has an internal mixer, there is also the option to pass the microphone signal directly from the input of the interface to the headphone output.

Figure 1.5

Chapter 2

INSTALLATION AND GETTING STARTED

Before Digital Performer can be used, it must be installed on the computer. This is a simple and quick procedure. Installation is a two-step process. First, the software is installed from a DVD to the system hard drive of the computer. The second step is to authorize Digital Performer to run on the computer. Once Digital Performer is installed and authorized, the software will be ready for use.

This chapter will describe what happens the first time Digital Performer is run on a computer. Creation of a new project will be described. Basic setup of MIDI and audio input and output will be described. Factory default preferences and user customizable preferences will also be discussed.

This chapter can be helpful if you ever have problems with the Digital Performer studio. Reviewing the information in this chapter will help you troubleshoot the basic configuration of the software and studio.

Installing Digital Performer

Digital Performer installs from a DVD disc. The software is copy protected, which means that once Digital Performer is installed on the computer, it cannot be copied from one hard drive to another.

On the Mac, it is possible to set up different user accounts. A user account may or may not be set to have Admin status. In order to install Digital Performer onto a Mac, the computer must be currently running under a user account that has Admin status. On both Mac and Windows computers, antivirus software can interfere with installation of software applications. It may be necessary to disable any antivirus software when installing Digital Performer.

When the Digital Performer DVD is inserted into the computer drive, a window will open on the desktop with an installer icon. Double-click on the installer icon and follow the instructions for installation.

When Digital Performer is installed onto a computer, there are many files that must be placed in specific locations. This is all handled by the installer. The Digital

Performer application is installed to the Applications folder on a Mac and into the Programs folder on a Windows computer.

The Digital Performer application installs to the primary system drive. When projects are created with Digital Performer, those projects can be created and stored to any hard drive that is connected to the computer.

Authorizing Digital Performer

Once installation is complete, it is time to launch Digital Performer. The first time that Digital Performer is launched, it will go through a procedure to complete its authorization on the hard drive. Part of the authorization involves Digital Performer communicating with the MOTU Internet server. In order to authorize Digital Performer directly, the computer must be connected to the Internet. If the computer is not connected to the Internet, the authorization procedure will generate a file. This file can be transferred to a computer that is connected to the Internet.

Double-click on the Digital Performer shortcut or application icon. A window will open that asks for an e-mail address and a key code. The key code is on a sticker on the inside rear cover of the Digital Performer manual. Enter the code exactly, including hyphens.

Once the e-mail address and key code have been entered, press the OK button. Digital Performer will communicate with the MOTU Internet server. The authorization will be completed and Digital Performer will open.

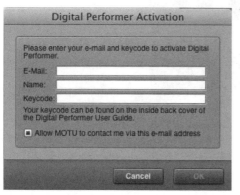

Figure 2.1

If the computer is not connected to the Internet, a window will open that provides the option to save or load an authorization challenge file.

Save the challenge file. The file will then need to be moved to a computer that is connected to the Internet. On the connected computer, launch a web browser and go to the following address: http://auth.motu.com.

The MOTU server will open with a window that allows the authorization challenge file to be uploaded.

Figure 2.2

Once the authorization challenge file is uploaded, the server will respond with a challenge response file. The challenge response file can then be moved back to the Digital Performer computer, and loaded in to complete the authorization.

Figure 2.4

Figure 2.3

Launching Digital Performer

Double-click on the Digital Performer shortcut or application icon to launch the software. It is also possible to double-click on a Digital Performer session file icon to launch the software and open that file directly.

When Digital Performer is launched, the first thing that appears is a splash screen with the DP8 logo. As the program opens, it initializes the MIDI system, and then the audio system. On the splash screen, text will scroll by as the individual effects and instrument plug-ins are loaded.

Select VST or Audio Unit on Mac

The first time that Digital Performer is launched on an Apple computer, a window will open that asks the operator to select VST or Audio Units as the default format for third-party audio plug-ins. Once the selection is made, this window will not open again. Digital Performer does not display this window when launched under Windows.

Many plug-in developers release their plug-ins in multiple formats. Digital Performer can run both Audio Unit and VST plug-ins under Mac. It is confusing to have both versions of the plug-in loaded at the same time. Therefore, on a Mac computer, Digital Performer provides the initial preference to select the default format for third-party plug-ins.

The stock plug-ins that are installed with Digital Performer are MAS format. The stock MAS plug-ins are common to Mac and Windows systems.

VST is a common plug-in format for Mac and Windows. If a Digital Performer session file is moved between a Mac and Windows system, and both systems have the same VST plug-ins installed, the session file will remember its VST plug-in assignments when moved between platforms. Select VST as the default format if there is any possibility that the session file will be moved to a Windows system.

Older versions of Digital Performer do not support VST format plug-ins. Therefore, older-version session files will be missing any third-party plug-ins if the Audio Unit plug-ins have been replaced by VST versions. Select Audio Unit as the default format if it is likely that files created in older versions of Digital Performer will be opened in this current version.

Digital Performer has an audio plug-in manager in Preferences > General > Audio Plug-Ins. The plug-in manager lists all available plug-ins, including listing their formats. MAS, VST, and Audio Unit plug-ins can be enabled or disabled at any time via the audio plug-in manager.

Open/New File Window

The factory default preference is that Digital Performer will launch and display a standard Open File dialog box. This window is a Mac or Windows window that allows the operator to open an existing Digital Performer session file.

To create a new Digital Performer project on the Mac, press the New button. This will open a standard New File dialog box.

The Windows Open File dialog box does not provide a New button. Therefore, on Windows, press the Cancel button; then, in the Digital Performer window, go to the File menu and choose New > New. This will open the New File dialog box.

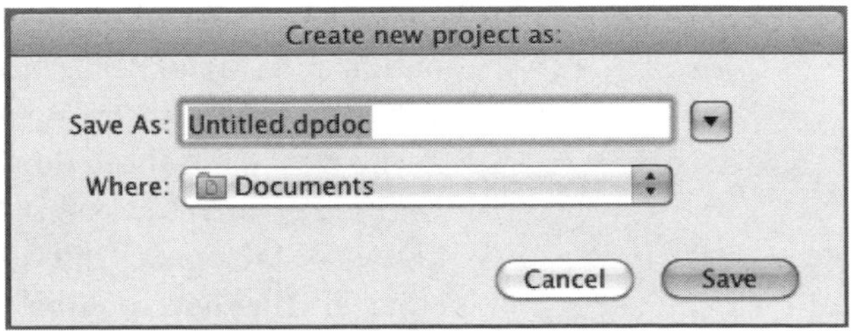

Figure 2.5

There are two things that must be done when creating a new Digital Performer project. The new project must be named, and a location on a hard drive must be selected. The Digital Performer project can be saved to any location on any hard drive that is connected to the computer.

Create a New Project

When a new project is named and saved, Digital Performer creates a directory on the computer hard drive called a project folder. If the new project is named Opus #7, for example, Digital Performer creates a directory folder called Opus #7 Project.

Inside the project folder, Digital Performer creates the actual session file. The session file contains tracks, automation, and MIDI data. A session file is identified with a DP icon.

When Digital Performer records audio, it creates sound files. The sound files are separate from the session file. The session file references the sound files. The sound files themselves are initially created and placed into a subfolder in the project folder called Audio Files.

Figure 2.6

Digital Performer has the ability to remember every edit made in a session. This information is stored as an undo history. The actual record of edits is stored inside the session file. However, if edit events involve audio, sound files that are referenced by the undo history are stored in a subfolder in the project folder called Undo.

There are potentially multiple files involved in a Digital Performer project. In addition to the session file, audio files, and undo history, there may be movie files and other types of files associated with the project. To keep things as organized as possible, the project folder is used as a container for all files associated with the project.

The key to starting a new Digital Performer project is to be organized. Pay attention to where the new session and its project folder are created. For the first session, go ahead and save to the desktop of the computer. The project folder can be moved later. Saving the first new project to the desktop will make it very easy to find that project and see its contents.

One last word on creating a new session: Don't use nonstandard text characters for file names. For example, the Mac and Windows operating systems see characters such as the forward-slash and backslash as programming information. Never use a forward slash or backslash as part of a file name. Stick to standard text characters for file names. This includes audio file names.

Default New File Template

Once the new session file has been named, choose a save location. Press the Save button and Digital Performer will open with a default new file session template.

What initially shows up onscreen is a factory default setup of the new file. Digital Performer is not limited to this file setup every time a new session is created. The Digital Performer session can be customized and saved as a new file template. As a matter of fact, once Digital Performer is running, check under File > New, to get a submenu that lists multiple factory templates. Also in the File menu, there is an option to Save As Template. If a session file is customized and saved as a new file template, it will appear in the File menu under New as a template option.

The factory default new file template opens with a single window. The new file initially displays the Consolidated window, which includes the Control Panel and Tracks windows.

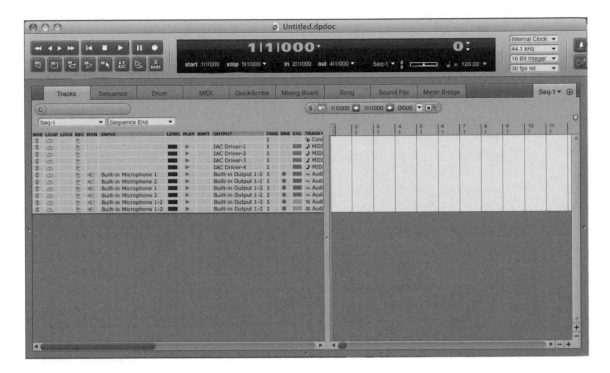

Figure 2.7

The Consolidated window will open with MIDI and audio tracks ready to use. The factory default template includes four MIDI tracks, four mono audio tracks, and two stereo audio tracks.

Besides the window layout and track configuration, there are many other settings that are defaults in the new file. For example, the meter is set to 4/4 time and tempo is set to 120 bpm. The default key signature for a default new file is C major. All these settings can be customized and saved as a new file template.

Preferences

Digital Performer is a highly customizable program. The interface of Digital Performer can be configured to show or hide only what the operator wants to see. There are many choices with regard to the user interface and workflow of the program.

There are many ways to customize the interface and functions of Digital Performer. These customizations are done via the Preferences window. On the Mac, the Preferences window is located in the Digital Performer menu. On Windows, Preferences is located in the Edit menu. The default key command to open the Preferences window is Command + , (comma).

Because there are so many options, it is necessary to start with factory default preferences. Factory default preferences are settings within Digital Performer that have been made by MOTU. What is initially displayed when Digital Performer is run for the first time is based on the factory default preferences. The factory default preferences can be changed at any time.

To reset the factory preferences in Digital Performer, press the Default button at the bottom of the Preferences window. To revert to preference settings that have just been changed, press the Revert button.

It is worth spending the time to look through all the options in the Preferences window. Doing so will reveal a great deal about how the program works and what options there are for customization of the interface and workflow.

For example, in the Preferences window, go to Display > Themes. In the Themes preferences, there are presets for different "skins" for Digital Performer. These preset themes change the visual look of the software. Click through a few of the Theme presets, and the changes will be obvious.

For a different example, Digital Performer can record audio files with a WAV or an AIFF format. Set the default audio file type in the Preferences window under General > Audio Files. This particular preference allows the audio file type to be set for this project only, as well as setting the default file type for all new projects that are created.

Configure Audio Input and Output

In order to record and play back MIDI and audio signals, inputs and outputs for those signals must be configured. The following section describes how to configure input and output to Digital Performer for audio and MIDI.

The Audio Hardware Driver

In order to record and play audio, Digital Performer must have audio inputs and outputs available. The factory default preference of Digital Performer is to use the built-in audio hardware of the computer. If there is a separate audio interface connected to the computer, Digital Performer must be configured to use that interface instead of the built-in audio ports of the computer. The audio input and output of Digital Performer is configured under Setup > Configure Audio System > Configure Hardware Driver.

The Mac OS uses a single driver type

Figure 2.8

called a Core Audio Driver. On the Mac, any audio input and output used by Digital Performer goes through a Core Audio Driver. Therefore, if the Configure Hardware Driver window in DP is opened on a Mac, the choices for input and output all use the same Core Audio driver type. If there is no additional audio hardware connected to the Mac, the choices in the Configure Hardware Driver window will be limited to the built-in audio inputs and outputs of the computer.

If there is an external audio interface connected to and communicating with the computer, that hardware will be available as a choice in the Configure Hardware Driver window.

Figure 2.9

Windows supports two major audio driver types. The Microsoft driver standard is called WDM. There is also another widely used driver type that is called ASIO. ASIO is a proprietary format originally developed by the Steinberg Media Technologies (the developers of Cubase and Nuendo software). ASIO has been widely adopted by other software and hardware developers. The reason that ASIO exists is because it has some technical capabilities that are not found in the Microsoft WDM driver type.

Under Windows, Digital Performer can use either WDM or ASIO as its audio driver format. Which driver type is used will be determined by the audio hardware. Any built-in sound card on a Windows computer will be supported by WDM, but may not be supported by ASIO. If the sound card in the computer is not supported by ASIO, Digital Performer will work with the sound card via WDM. If the built-in sound card or external audio interface is supported by both WDM and ASIO, ASIO is generally the preferred driver type.

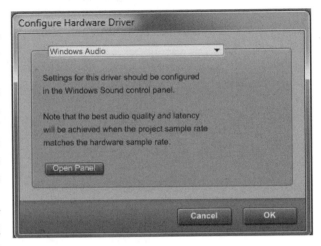

Therefore, in the Audio Hardware Driver window on Windows, first choose which driver type Digital Performer will use, and then choose the actual audio hardware to be accessed by that driver. By default on Windows, Digital Performer will be assigned to a WDM driver and to the available sound card in the computer.

Figure 2.10

In Fig. 2.11, ASIO has been selected as the driver format. In this example, a MOTU MicroBook interface is connected to a Windows computer, and is configured to work with Digital Performer.

Once the audio interface or built-in audio ports are selected, close the Audio Hardware Driver window. Digital Performer will now use the selected audio I/O for recording and playback.

Always power-on the audio interface before Digital Performer is launched. If Digital Performer launches and the audio interface is not communicating with the computer, Digital Performer will revert back to using the computer's built-in audio inputs and outputs. If that happens, reset the audio hardware driver. If Digital Performer ever loses connection with audio inputs and outputs, go back to the Audio Hardware Driver window and recheck the settings.

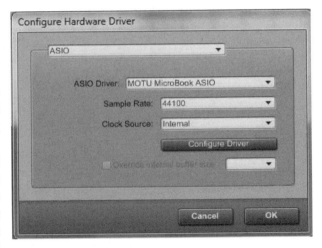

Figure 2.11

If the external audio interface is not listed in the Audio Hardware Driver window, then that means the interface is not communicating with the computer. Quit Digital Performer while troubleshooting the interface. Check to make sure that any available drivers for the interface are installed. Check the cable connections. Check any configuration software that may come with the audio interface. Once the audio interface is properly communicating with the computer, it will be available to Digital Performer.

In addition to selecting the audio hardware device for Digital Performer, the Audio Hardware Driver window has additional settings for clock source, sample rate, and buffer size. For now, leave these settings alone. Later in this book, I will discuss what these settings do and when to change them.

Audio Track Inputs and Outputs

To be the master of the studio, having an understanding of signal flow is critical. Recording audio into Digital Performer requires that you have a path for that signal that goes into the software. For example, there may be a microphone that is plugged into the audio interface. The audio interface is then connected to the computer. That provides the physical path for the signal. Assuming that the audio interface is communicating with the computer and is configured to work with Digital Performer, the next step is to configure inputs and outputs to an audio track.

An audio track must have a working output in order to play back. An audio track must have a working input and output in order to record.

The same setting can often be made in more than one place inside Digital Performer. For example, audio track inputs and outputs can be assigned in the Mixing Board window, the Tracks window, and the Sequence Editor window.

In the Tracks window, there is a column for Input and a separate column for Output. Track inputs and outputs are assigned separately.

In the Sequence Editor, inputs and outputs are assigned via pop-up menus on the left edge of the track. If the pop-up menus are not visible, expand the Track view vertically.

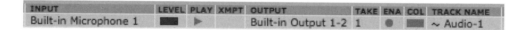

Figure 2.12

In the Mixing Board window, track inputs and outputs can be assigned at the bottom of each fader strip.

Typically, all the audio tracks will have the same initial output assignment. Usually, the Output column will display a stereo assignment that represents the stereo audio output from the computer. For example, if you are using the built-in audio outputs, the following figure shows what the audio track output assignment will be:

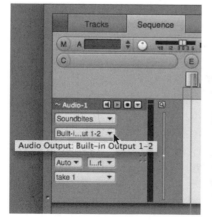

Figure 2.13

Figure 2.14

If the output assignment is displayed in italics, that means the track has lost its assignment. The output must be reassigned, or else the track will not play back or record. Click-and-hold on the output assignment field of the track, and a menu will be displayed. If the desired output

T	OUTPUT	TAKE	ENA	COL	TRACK NAME
	Built-in Output 1-2	1	●	▬	~ Audio-1
	Built-in Output 1-2	1	●	▬	~ Audio-2
	Built-in Output 1-2	1	●	▬	~ Audio-3
	Built-in Output 1-2	1	●	▬	~ Audio-4
	Built-in Output 1-2	1	●	▬	≈ Audio-5
	Built-in Output 1-2	1	●	▬	≈ Audio-6

Figure 2.15

pair is not visible in the menu, choose New Mono or Stereo Bundle and all currently available audio outputs will be shown in a list. Choose the correct output pair, and that assignment will now be available as an output assignment for all audio tracks.

For track inputs, check the Input column. If an assignment appears in italics, that means the input must be reassigned. Click-and-hold on the track input to get a menu. If the desired input is not visible, choose New Mono Bundle or New Stereo Bundle (depending on the track type). The submenu will provide choices for all the available audio inputs.

To record a mono signal, use a mono audio track with a mono input. To record a stereo audio signal, use a stereo audio track with stereo audio input. It is not possible to assign a mono input to a stereo track. It is not possible to assign a stereo input to a mono track.

Check Input Level

Once the input and output of the track is configured, the next step is to check the input level of the signal that is to be recorded. Make sure that the input level is neither too loud nor too soft. This is done by checking the Audio Monitor window. Open the Audio Monitor window from the Studio menu, the shortcut, or a sidebar. The default key command to open the Audio Monitor window is Shift + A.

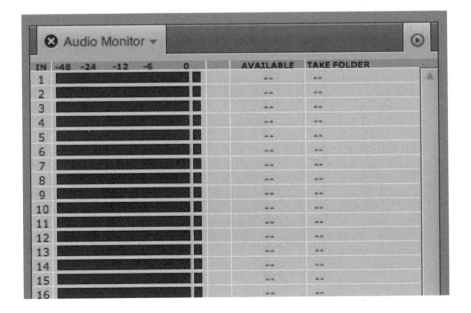

Figure 2.16

To check audio level coming into a track, the track must be record-armed. Tracks can be record-armed from within different windows. In the Tracks window, look for the buttons in the REC column.

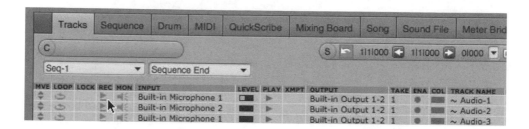

Figure 2.17

In the Sequence Editor, the Record-arm button is in the left edge of each track.
In the Mixing Board window, the Record-arm button is above the fader and panner.

Once the track is armed, a corresponding volume meter in the Audio Monitor window will be highlighted. If there is any audio signal present at the input of the audio track, there will be activity in the VU meter of the Audio Monitor window.

If signal appears in the VU meter, then that means everything is set up correctly up to that point. The next step is to adjust the volume of the input signal for an ideal recording level. Input volume is not set from within Digital Performer. Input level is set on the audio interface, or from whatever device is sending signal into the interface. If a microphone is plugged directly into an audio interface, change the preamp gain on the interface to get a good recording level.

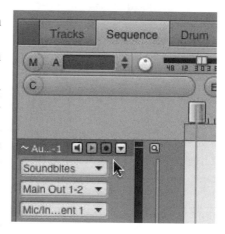

Figure 2.18

Generally, there should be as much signal in the VU meter as possible, without overloading the input. Overloading the input will cause clipping distortion.

There is a red clip indicator on the Audio Monitor VU meter. If the red light is lit, that means the input signal has overloaded at some point. To clear the clip indicator, press Command + / (backslash) on the computer keyboard.

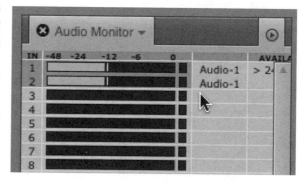

Figure 2.20

Figure 2.19

Audio Input Monitoring

For a musician to make music, he or she generally needs to be able to hear the sounds that are being produced. In some cases, the musician hears the instrument naturally. For example, a violinist doesn't need headphones or speakers to hear the violin's sound.

If the job is to record a solo violinist, no additional monitor speakers or headphones may be required. As a matter of fact, a monitoring system is not required at all to record a signal. It is possible to just check the input level and press the Record button.

At some point, however, it is likely that the musicians and recording engineer will need to be able to monitor both live input signals and playback from Digital Performer. For example, if the violinist wants to play along to prerecorded tracks and monitor with a pair of headphones, now he or she does need a working audio monitor system. As was discussed in an earlier chapter there are two basic ways to monitor live audio signals with a DAW. Live signals can be monitored directly from input to output through the audio interface. Live signals can also be monitored through Digital Performer.

The reason you would want to monitor a live audio signal through Digital Performer is if the live signal were to be monitored through a software plug-in effect. For example, if guitar-processing plug-ins are being run within Digital Performer, a guitar signal can be sent through those effects for live monitoring of the processed signal.

The reason you would want to monitor a live signal with direct hardware monitoring would be if there were no CPU latency delay added to that monitored signal, and the monitoring path didn't place any processing load on the computer CPU.

In a DAW setup some audio signals may be monitored directly from input to output, while other signals may be monitored through Digital Performer and the effects plug-ins. What should be avoided is monitoring the same signal through both paths at the same time.

By default, Digital Performer is set up to use direct input monitoring if possible. The "if possible" part means that in order for direct input monitoring to work, there has to be a hardware path for that signal. Some external audio interfaces support direct hardware monitoring. Some external audio interfaces do not have direct hardware monitoring capabilities, or they have some sort of hardware mixer that is not controllable from the computer. The built-in audio jacks of the computer do not support direct hardware monitoring.

Check to see if direct hardware monitoring is available with your current system. In Digital Performer, go to Setup > Configure Audio System > Input Monitoring Mode.

If Direct Hardware Playthrough is not an available option, then that means Digital Performer is not connected to audio hardware with that capability. If the audio hardware does not have direct monitoring capabilities, Digital Performer will default to monitoring through the computer.

In the Input Monitoring Mode window, select Monitor Record-Enabled Tracks Through Effects.

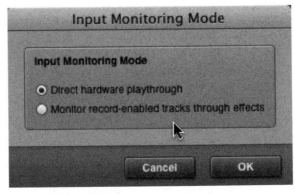

Figure 2.21

That will enable external audio signals to be passed through Digital Performer and therefore through live plug-in effects.

If the option to Monitor Record-Enabled Tracks Through Effects is selected, the option to use direct hardware monitoring is still available, as long as the audio interface has that capability. When Digital Performer is set to monitor through the computer, any direct hardware monitoring has to be set up separately. For example, the audio interface may have a separate software application to configure a direct monitor mix. That mix can be run at the same time as Digital Performer is patching other signals through the computer.

Once input monitoring mode is selected, close the window. Go to the Studio menu and choose Audio Patch Thru > Auto.

If direct hardware monitoring is available and selected, the record-enabled audio track will now patch a signal through from input to output. If speakers or headphones are connected to the output of the interface, the output signal will play back. If a live microphone is connected, watch out for feedback from the speakers!

If the live input signal is not present in the monitors at this point, check the signal path from beginning to end. Is there a signal coming into the audio interface? Is there a track in Digital Performer that is assigned to the correct input

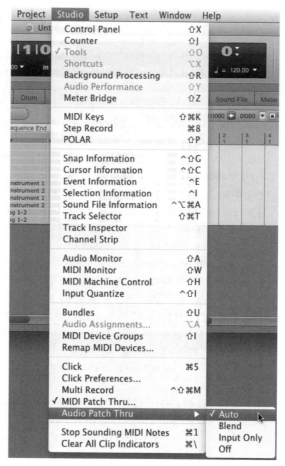

Figure 2.22

on the audio interface? Is that track record-armed? Is the input level showing up in the Audio Monitor window? Is Audio Patch Thru set to Auto? Is there any output activity on the audio interface? Is the output of the audio interface (or the computer monitor volume) turned up?

Latency Delay

The downside of monitoring through Digital Performer is that when a signal is patched through a computer, the computer delays the signal. This is known as "latency delay." The delay of the monitored signal can be adjusted so that it is undetectable to the ear. The delay time is adjustable via a software setting in the audio hardware driver. The quicker the patch-through, the harder the computer has to work. It is possible to patch a signal though fast enough that any delay will be inaudible to the ear. However, that job will tax the CPU power of the computer.

In Digital Performer, go to Setup > Configure Audio System > Configure Hardware Driver. In this window the setting will control latency delay. The lower the buffer size setting, the quicker the patch-through and the greater the load on the CPU.

To monitor live audio through Digital Performer, start with a buffer size of 256. If the monitored input signal still feels like there is a delay, try a buffer setting of 128. For the quickest possible patch-through, drop down to a setting of 64. If the computer runs out of CPU power, Digital Performer will put up an error message. If that happens, cut back on the number of live effects that are running, or raise the buffer size.

The reason buffer size is variable is because there are times when low latency is required, and other times when monitoring latency is not an issue. When monitoring live audio through Digital Performer, or when triggering virtual instruments from an external MIDI controller, the buffer size needs to be set to a low level to avoid latency delay. During mixdown, it is advantageous to set the buffer size to its maximum setting in order to ease the load on the CPU.

It is important to understand that latency delay is an issue only of live monitoring. Latency delay is not an issue when playing back MIDI, audio, or instrument tracks within Digital Performer.

Test Audio Recording

When signal level is present in the Audio Monitor window, the track is ready to record audio. Press the Record button in the Control Panel window. The counter will roll, and the green cursor will move from left to right. Send signal to the track input, and audio will record into the track. Press the Stop button in the Transport window.

If a file gets recorded but a waveform does not appear in the file, that suggests that there is no audio input to the track. Check the input assignment of the track. Check the Audio Monitor window to make sure that signal is getting into Digital Performer from the live input.

Test Audio Playback

Press the Rewind button in the Control Panel. It is also possible to grab the top of the playback cursor and position it manually. Press Play. The cursor will pass over the recorded waveform. At that point there should be audible playback. If audio is heard when playing back a track, that means the audio system is set up and working.

If a waveform has been recorded but there is no audible playback, follow the signal chain out of Digital Performer. Is the output assignment for the track correct? Is the track play-enabled? Check the audio interface. Is the output volume turned up? Are the speakers turned on and connected to the correct outputs on the interface?

Configure MIDI Input and Output

Digital Performer can record and play back MIDI information. MIDI is not sound. MIDI is computer control information. That control information can be used to do many things, including triggering a piece of hardware or software to make sound. MIDI can be generated directly from within Digital Performer, or from an external hardware controller device.

MIDI can be used to trigger sounds in hardware devices or in software programs. A piece of software that generates sound when triggered by MIDI is called a virtual instrument. A studio may use a combination of hardware sound modules and virtual instruments. In order to use external MIDI devices with Digital Performer, there needs to be a path for the MIDI signal to go from the MIDI controller into the software. There also needs to be a path for the MIDI signal to go out of Digital Performer into any hardware sound modules.

When playing on a MIDI keyboard or MIDI drum pads, for example, that device generates MIDI information. In some cases, the keyboard or MIDI drum pads may also have a built-in sound module. This type of device requires two-way MIDI communication. MIDI from the controller comes into Digital Performer. The sound module receives MIDI from Digital Performer. Typically, with a device that is both controller and sound module, there is an internal parameter in that device called Local Control, which should be disabled when using that device with Digital Performer.

It is also possible to have a device that generates MIDI but does not have any internal sound-generating capabilities. An example of this could be a MIDI controller keyboard or drum pads that do not include a sound-generator module. This type of device only needs one-way communication to send MIDI information into Digital Performer.

A device that is a dedicated sound module also only needs one-way communication. There needs to be a path for the MIDI signal from Digital Performer out to that external device.

Configure MIDI Devices

Part of the setup of Digital Performer involves creating a configuration map of all external MIDI devices that are connected to the computer. This includes MIDI devices that connect to the computer via USB, as well as any hardware MIDI interfaces and devices connected to a MIDI interface.

On a Mac, Digital Performer uses the Apple Audio MIDI Setup utility for its MIDI configuration. Any interfaces or devices configured in Apple Audio MIDI Setup will be reflected in Digital Performer. There is no utility similar to the Apple Audio MIDI Setup for Windows.

On Mac and Windows, the Digital Performer MIDI configuration can be set up by going to Studio > Bundles, and then clicking on the MIDI Devices tab.

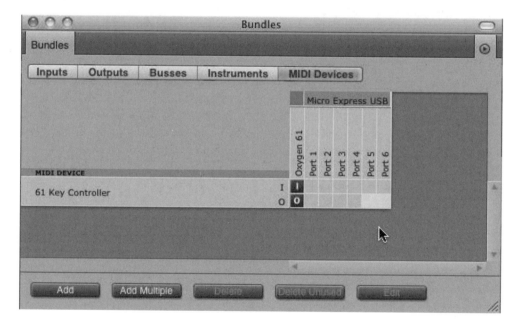

Figure 2.23

Initially, the MIDI Devices tab in the Bundles window will display any MIDI interfaces or USB MIDI devices that are connected to the computer. Press the Add button to create a new external device. The external device represents a controller or sound module that is connected to a MIDI interface. Double-click on the new external device to get a MIDI Device Properties window. Click on the Manufacturer pop-up menu to choose the manufacturer. Click on the Model pop-up menu to select the device from that manufacturer.

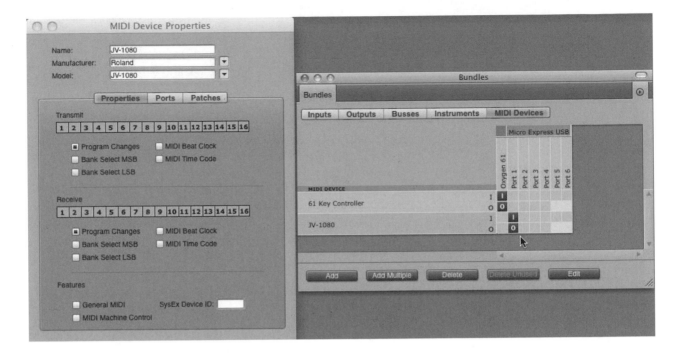

Figure 2.24

If the model or manufacturer for a specific device does not show up in the list, enter the name of the device in the name field. Move the I/O icons for the newly created MIDI device to the appropriate input and output ports on the MIDI interface.

Follow this procedure for each external MIDI device until the Bundles window correctly lists all connected external MIDI devices. Digital Performer relies on the accuracy of this configuration to send and receive MIDI through the correct interface ports for each external MIDI device.

Patch Lists for External MIDI Devices

Digital Performer can display patch lists for configured MIDI devices. External MIDI devices are configured in the Bundles window in Digital Performer. On the Mac, external MIDI devices can also be configured in the Apple Audio MIDI Setup utility.

When DP8 is installed on a Mac or Windows computer, device descriptions and patch lists are also installed. If a manufacturer or model is not available in the Device Properties window in the Bundles window, then that means there is no listing for that manufacturer or device in the installed files. In some cases, there may be a listing for a device, but there may be no patch list available for that device. If there is no installed patch list for a MIDI device, Digital Performer will display a generic patch list that is numbered 1 through128, but has no patch names or bank select functions.

On the Mac, the device descriptions and patch lists are installed in the following location: Hard drive > Library > Audio > MIDI Devices > MOTU. On Windows, the device descriptions and patch lists are installed in this location: C Drive > Program Files > Common Files > MOTU > MIDI Devices.

If there is no device description or patch list available for a specific MIDI device, it is possible to create that information so that it is available to DP8.

Device descriptions are listed in documents with the file extension of .middev. Patch list documents use the extension of .midnam.

There needs to be only one .middev file for each manufacturer. There must be a separate .midnam file for each device from that manufacturer. In order for a .midnam patch list file to work, it must be referenced from a .middev file.

The .middev and .midnam files can be created, opened, and edited by a simple text editor application. The syntax within the document must be exactly correct, or else the document will not work.

The easiest way to create a new .midnam patch list file is to copy an existing .midnam file and modify that. Many manufacturers of MIDI devices use common patch list setups for all models. In some cases, patch list names may be common for multiple models from the same manufacturer.

The .midnam patch list format is used by other developers, and in some cases, there may be a .midnam file that has already been created and is available for download.

MIDI Monitor Window

A simple way to check if MIDI input is reaching Digital Performer is to record-arm a MIDI track, press Record in the Control Panel, and tap a few notes on the MIDI controller. If MIDI data records into the track it will be visible, and that will confirm that there is a working path for MIDI from the controller into Digital Performer.

The MIDI Monitor window can also be used to check MIDI input signal. Open the MIDI Monitor from the Studio menu, by using the shortcut button, or as a sidebar in the Consolidated window. The default key command to open the MIDI Monitor window is Shift + W.

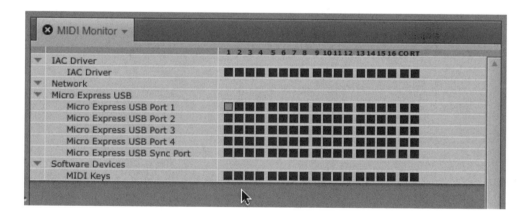

Figure 2.25

If the MIDI Monitor indicator lights up when the external MIDI controller is played, that confirms that MIDI is getting to the input of Digital Performer. If there is no activity in the MIDI Monitor when the external controller is played, that is a reliable indicator that no MIDI signal is reaching Digital Performer. If that's the case, check the signal flow from the controller into the computer.

MIDI Keys

It's possible to use the mouse or computer keyboard to generate MIDI notes. This can be helpful for testing signal flow or checking sounds. Open the MIDI Keys window from the Studio menu. When the MIDI Keys window is open, the keys on the computer keyboard are reassigned to trigger MIDI notes from within Digital Performer. It is also possible to click directly on the MIDI Keys window with the mouse. If there is a record-enabled MIDI track, it will receive the signal from MIDI Keys. If there is a software or hardware MIDI module receiving MIDI data from the record-enabled MIDI track, the MIDI Keys will trigger that instrument.

Signal Flow from MIDI to Audio

Here is a typical signal flow: MIDI is generated by an external controller (such as a keyboard, drum pads, guitar-to-MIDI converter, and so on). That MIDI is passed into the computer via a direct USB connection, or through a MIDI interface. If the direct USB connection or MIDI interface is configured properly, Digital Performer will be ready to receive the incoming MIDI signal.

For Digital Performer to pass a MIDI signal to an external sound module or an internal virtual instrument, there must be a MIDI track in the sequence, and that MIDI track must be record-armed. By default, Digital Performer is in omni receive mode. That means Digital Performer will record any MIDI signal that comes into the computer, regardless of MIDI channel or input port on the MIDI interface.

Once the MIDI track is record-armed, it will pass any incoming MIDI data to its assigned output. That output could be an internal virtual instrument or it could be an external hardware sound module. If the output of the track is assigned and the hardware or software instrument is configured correctly, live MIDI data will pass from the external controller, through the record-enabled MIDI track, and to the assigned output of the track. To hear sound, the next step is to follow the audio signal path from the software instrument or hardware module through to the audio monitor system.

Create a Virtual Instrument

Digital Performer ships with a basic set of virtual instruments. The Mac and Windows operating systems also have a built-in virtual instrument that provides a palette of sounds that conform to the General MIDI specification. It's also possible to install virtual instruments made by other companies into Digital Performer. On a Mac, Digital Performer works with virtual instruments that support the MAS, Audio Unit, and VST plug-in formats. On a Windows computer, Digital Performer works with MAS and VST format plug-ins.

Because a virtual instrument runs as a plug-in inside Digital Performer, it's actually simpler to set up than it is to set up an external sound module.

To add a virtual instrument plug-in to the Digital Performer session, go to the Project menu and choose Add Track > Instrument Track. A submenu that shows a list of all currently available virtual instruments will be available.

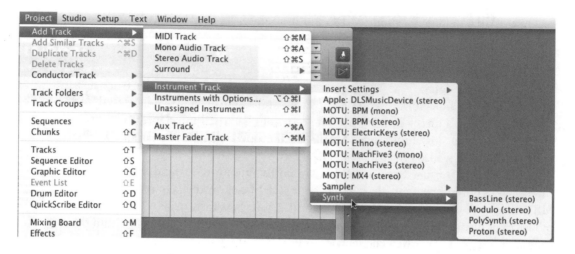

Figure 2.26

Once a virtual instrument is selected from the menu, a window will open to show the controls for that instrument. If the instrument uses audio samples to generate sound, it may be necessary to load a sample into the instrument. If the instrument is a synthesizer, a patch may need to be loaded.

With the exception of Model 12 and Nanosampler, the virtual instruments included with Digital Performer are synthesizers. For all of the virtual instruments included with Digital Performer, patches or samples can be loaded via the menu in the upper left-hand corner of the plug-in window.

For a quick test, add a Bassline virtual instrument to the sequence, and choose a patch from the menu in the Bassline window.

When a virtual instrument is added to the sequence, Digital Performer creates an instrument track. The virtual instrument is set up as a device within that instrument track. Check in the Tracks window, or in any other window that

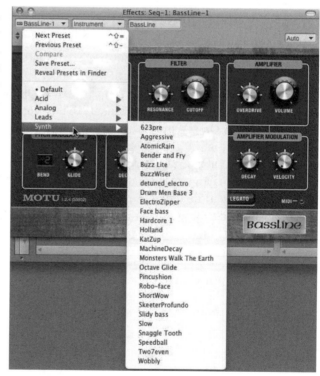

Figure 2.27

shows tracks in Digital Performer to see the new instrument track. The following figure shows a view of an instrument track in the Tracks window.

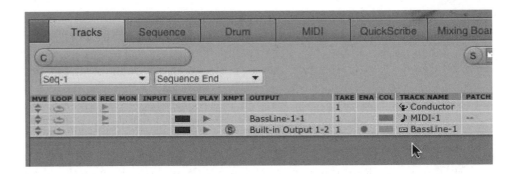

Figure 2.28

Notice that there is no input assignment for the Instrument track. An instrument track receives MIDI from a MIDI track. To get MIDI into an instrument track, there must be a MIDI track, and the output of the MIDI track must be assigned to the instrument track. For an Instrument track to be available as a MIDI output, that instrument track must exist in the sequence. In other words, if a Bassline instrument is not added to the sequence, Bassline will not be available as an output destination for MIDI tracks.

The output of the instrument track is an audio signal. Therefore, the output will be assigned to the audio monitor outputs.

Once the instrument and MIDI tracks are configured, then test signal flow. Record-arm a MIDI track. Set the output of the MIDI track to the virtual instrument. Play a note on the MIDI controller. If everything is set up correctly, the virtual instrument will generate sound that will be audible from the monitor speakers or the headphones. If there is no sound when playing on the controller keyboard, go back and check each step of the MIDI and audio signal path.

Test MIDI Record

Once the MIDI and audio signal paths are configured, then test signal flow. Record-arm a MIDI track. Set the output of the MIDI track to an external sound module. Play a note on the MIDI controller. If everything is set up correctly, the sound module will generate sound that is audible on the monitor speakers or the headphones. If there is no sound when playing on the MIDI controller, go back and check each step of the signal path, from MIDI input through to audio output.

Once the external MIDI sound module is connected to the computer and configured in Digital Performer, check the audio output of the external sound module. There needs to be a signal path from the audio output of the sound module to the audio monitor system. If an audio interface is being used that has a direct hardware monitor function, it is possible to connect the audio outputs of the sound module directly to the inputs of the audio interface. The audio interface can then patch that signal directly to the monitor outputs. Depending on how the audio interface works, it may be possible to set up a direct monitor path for the external sound module that is independent from Digital Performer.

If the audio interface does not have a direct hardware patch-through function and some sort of external mixer is not being used, it is possible to patch the external sound module through Digital Performer for live monitoring. To do that, go to the Project menu and choose Add Track > Aux Track. A new track will be added to the sequence. An aux track is used to pass audio from one place to another inside Digital Performer.

There are many uses for an aux track. To set up an aux track to monitor an external sound module, set the input of the aux track to the corresponding inputs on the audio interface. Set the output of the aux track to the monitor outputs. The aux track will now pass the signal from that input to that output. If an aux track is used to monitor an external audio signal, CPU latency delay will be introduced to that signal. To reduce patch-through delay, lower the buffer size in the Audio Hardware Driver window.

By now a MIDI track has been set up and its output has been assigned to either a virtual instrument or an external sound module. The MIDI track has been record-armed and signal flow has been tested from the MIDI controller to audio output. To record MIDI press the Record button in the Control Panel. Press Play on the MIDI controller. Sound should be audible and MIDI data should be recorded into the MIDI track. Press Stop in the Control Panel.

Test MIDI Playback

Press Rewind in the Control Panel. Press Play. As the playback wiper moves past the recorded MIDI data, the MIDI will data-trigger the virtual instrument or external sound module to send sound to the monitor speakers or the headphones.

Chapter 3

Navigating the Interface

This chapter describes the basic layout and interface of Digital Performer. Digital Performer uses windows to display information and controls. Digital Performer makes use of menus, tabs, shortcuts, customizable key and MIDI commands, and other techniques to control the software. This chapter will describe how to navigate between the primary windows and how to control the basic functions. By the end of this chapter, the reader will have a basic understanding of how to navigate and control Digital Performer.

The interface of Digital Performer is highly customizable. This chapter will describe how to use the Consolidated window to easily manage multiple windows. I will also describe how to create window sets and how to change the look of Digital Performer by using Themes.

Windows
Digital Performer makes extensive use of windows to display tools, data, and other functions. Windows are organized in a way to make the workflow as obvious as possible.

Managing Windows
There are multiple ways to open windows in Digital Performer. They can be opened by selecting them from menus. Windows can also be opened via key commands, remote MIDI commands, window tabs, and shortcut buttons.

It is possible to open many windows in Digital Performer. Depending on monitor space, windows can cover the computer desktop. It's also possible to simplify the interface of Digital Performer so that only the windows required for the job are visible. This is especially important when first learning the program.

MOTU has worked hard to make the interface of Digital Performer as easy to use as possible. For example, Digital Performer features something called the Consolidated window. The Consolidated window provides a single window open on the desktop, with all the essential functions of the program visible at a glance. The factory default new file opens to display the Consolidated window.

Window Tabs

Some windows in Digital Performer have tabs that provide additional options for the window. For example, the Consolidated window provides tabs to switch between the primary windows of the program.

Figure 3.1

Window Sets

It is possible to save a specific configuration of windows as a window set. Once all the Digital Performer windows are displayed as desired, go to the Window menu and choose Window Sets > Save Window Set. Name the window set and create a keyboard shortcut. It is possible to create as many window sets as needed. Notice that Digital Performer has several preset window sets already available in the Windows menu.

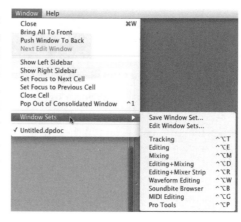

Menus

Digital Performer makes extensive use of menus for opening windows and controlling various functions. The main menus are at the top of the desktop on the Mac.

Figure 3.2

Figure 3.3

On Windows, the main menus are at the top of the Digital Performer window.

Figure 3.4

Many windows feature minimenus, which are available via a button in the upper right-hand corner of the window. For example, in the upper right-hand corner of the Mixing Board window, there is a minimenu that provides options for specific configuration changes to the mixer.

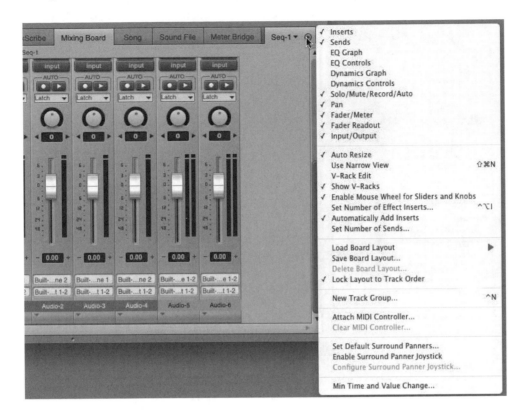

Figure 3.5

Figure 3.6

Some windows make use of pop-up menus. For example, in the Sequence Editor window, click-and-hold on the Insert pop-up menu to get a list of automation data types that can be inserted.

Most windows feature menus are available by right-clicking with the mouse. For example, right-click on a track fader in the Tracks window to get a menu with options that are specific to that track.

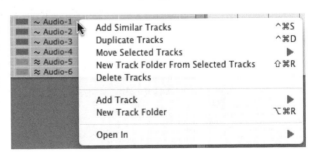

Figure 3.7

Shortcut Buttons

In addition to menu selections and tabs, windows can be opened by clicking on shortcut buttons. Shortcut buttons can be displayed as part of the Control Panel window. Shortcut buttons can also be displayed independently in their own window. The default preference of Digital Performer is to display the shortcut buttons in the

Control Panel window. This preference can be changed in Preferences > Display > Control Panel.

If the Shortcuts window is not displayed within the Control Panel window, it can be opened from the Studio menu.

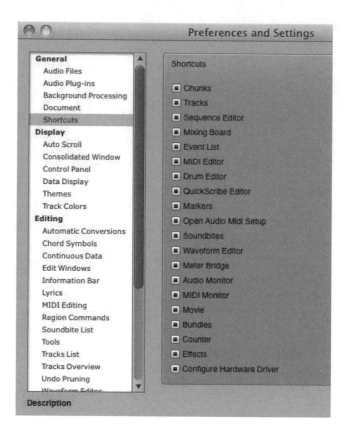

Figure 3.8

Specify which shortcut buttons are displayed via Preferences > General > Shortcuts.

Key Commands and MIDI Remote Control

Every window and function in Digital Performer can be mapped to a computer keyboard command. Additionally, all the same functions can be controlled via remote MIDI commands.

From the Setup menu, open the Commands window.

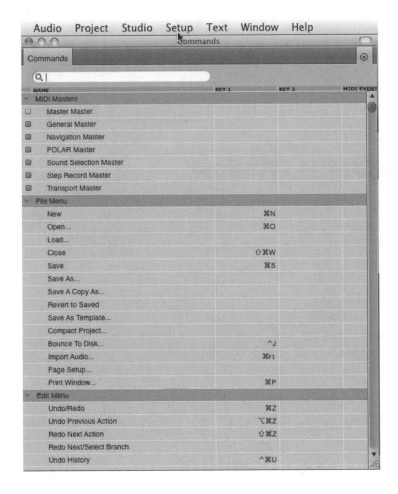

Figure 3.9

Commands are grouped in folders according to category. It is possible to create customized key command and MIDI remote control sets. Check the Commands window minimenu for these options.

The Commands window provides a search field for finding specific functions with Digital Performer. For example, type the word "play" to find all functions that include the word play.

MIDI remote control can be enabled or disabled. The very first item listed in the Commands window is labeled Master Master. Master Master is disabled by default. Enable Master Master by checking the box on the left. This enables MIDI remote control for Digital Performer.

Reassign a keyboard shortcut by clicking on the field and typing in the new command. If the key command is already in use for a different function, Digital Performer will display a message describing to which function the key command is currently assigned.

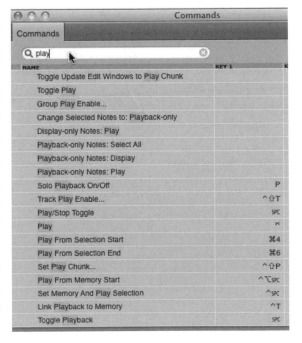

Figure 3.10

To assign a remote MIDI command to a function, click in the MIDI column for that function, and then send the external MIDI message. The Commands window will learn the MIDI command.

The contents of the Commands window can be printed. If a group of commands is hidden in a closed folder, it won't be included in the printout. That allows for printout of only specific commands. To print the contents of the Commands window, choose Print Window from the File menu.

The Consolidated Window

The Consolidated window provides a single window on the computer desktop that can contain one or many Digital Performer windows. The Consolidated window provides tabs, split windows, and sidebar windows to enable easy switching and display of the main windows within Digital Performer. The purpose of the Consolidated window is to simplify the user interface of Digital Performer.

The default new file opens to display the Consolidated window. In the factory default new file template, the Consolidated window initially opens to display the Control Panel window and the Tracks window.

It is important to understand that it is not a requirement to use the Consolidated window. The windows in Digital Performer can all be displayed separately. That can be useful when multiple video monitors are available and different windows are placed separately within the workspace.

It is possible to use the Consolidated window for some of the workspace and also have other windows that are displayed independently. For example, if two video monitors are available, it may be desirable to put the Mixing Board on one monitor and the Consolidated Window on the other.

As the user becomes more proficient with the software, the workplace can be further customized. As a new user to Digital Performer, start off using just the Consolidated window. This will keep the workspace uncluttered and more obvious to use.

Tabs

Along the top edge of the Consolidated window, there are a series of tabs. These tabs change which windows is currently displayed within the body of the Consolidated window. For example, click on the Mixing Board tab to display the Mixing Board window.

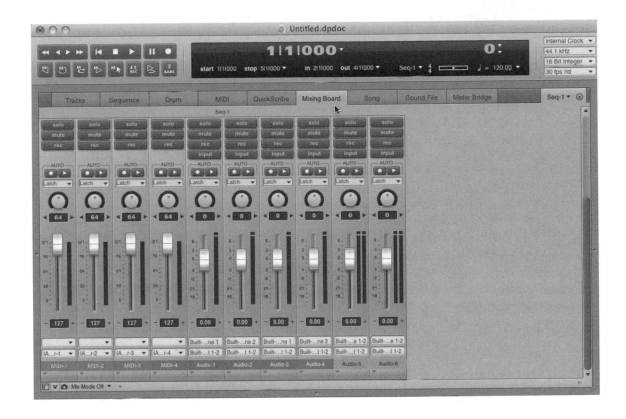

Figure 3.11

Click on the Tracks tab to display the Tracks window.

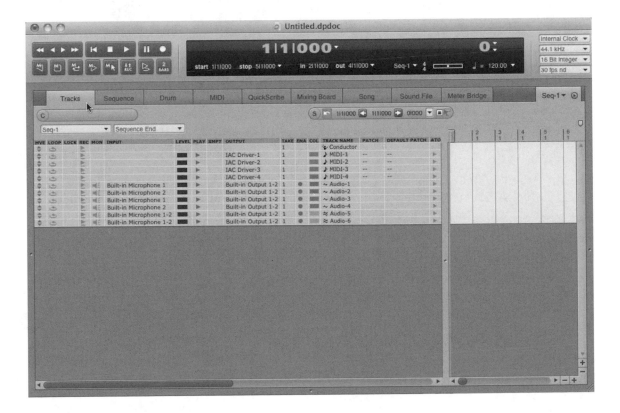

Figure 3.12

Display Multiple Windows

The Consolidated window can display more than one window at a time. The main body window can be split horizontally to display multiple windows, each with tabs. It is also possible to display windows in left and right sidebars within the Consolidated window.

Click on the very bottom edge of the Consolidated window and drag up. Alternately, double-click on the bottom edge of the Consolidated window. A new body window will be created inside the Consolidated window, with its own set of tabs. For example, display the Tracks window in the top half of the Consolidated window, and the Mixing Board window in the bottom half.

Figure 3.13

Click on the right or left edge of the Consolidated window and drag horizontally. Alternately, double-click on the right or left edge of the Consolidated window. This will create a sidebar window. There will be a single tab at the top of the sidebar with the name of the currently displayed window. Click on that name to get a menu of other windows. This allows switching between different displayed windows in the sidebar. For example, view the Audio Monitor window, then change that view to the Markers window. There is also a choice to view multiple windows in the sidebar window. Once a sidebar window has been created, add more windows to the sidebar by dragging (or double-clicking on) the bottom edge of the sidebar. Additional sidebar windows can also be created as selectable tabs. Do this from the menu at the top of the sidebar.

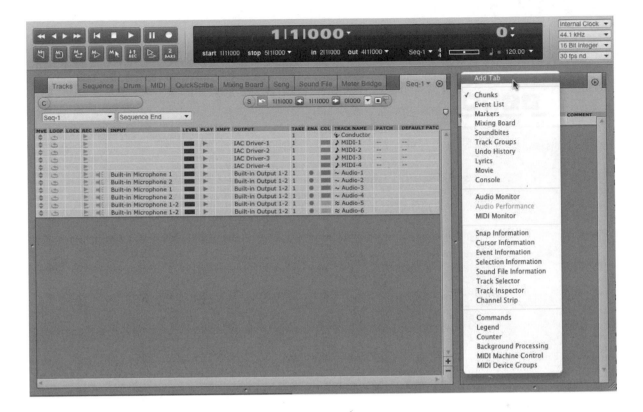

Figure 3.14

Separating Windows

To separate a window from the Consolidated window, click on the top edge of the window and drag it out of the Consolidated window. Alternately, go to the Window menu and choose Pop Out Of Consolidated Window.

Consolidated Window Preferences

In the Digital Performer Preferences window, go to Display > Consolidated Window. These settings customize how the Consolidated window works. For example, to always open the Mixing Board window as an independent window, deselect the Mixing Board in the Consolidated window Preferences area.

The Control Panel

The Control Panel window provides control of the Digital Performer sequence. There are Rewind, Stop, Pause, Play, and Record buttons. There are also other transport-related buttons and controls.

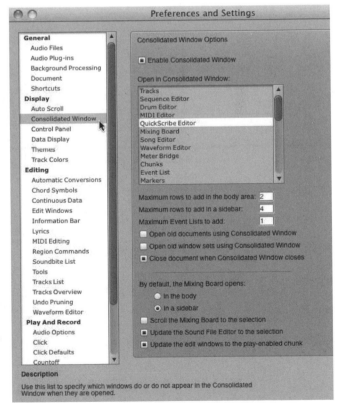

Figure 3.15

The Control Panel window displays two counters, which are used to show the current time location in the sequence. These counters can be configured to show sequence time in bars and beats, real time (minutes and seconds), SMPTE frame time, and numbers of audio samples. The two counters

Figure 3.16

allow two different time formats to be viewed simultaneously. Click on the arrow to the right of each counter to change the displayed time format.

Figure 3.17

The Control Panel can also be configured to show or hide shortcut buttons and editing tools. The Control Panel display can be customized in the Digital Performer Preferences under Display > Control Panel.

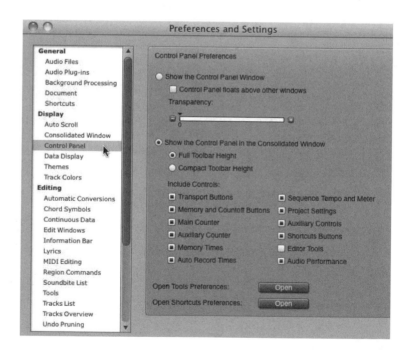

Figure 3.18

Editing Tools

The Tools window is used to display editing tools. Tools can also be displayed within the Control Panel window. The factory default preference of Digital Performer is to display Tools in the Control Panel window. Change this preference in Preferences > Display > Control Panel.

If the Tools window is not displayed within the Control Panel window, it can be opened from the Studio menu or via key command or MIDI command. The factory default key command to open the Tools window is Shift + O.

Which tools are displayed can be specified in Preferences > Editing > Tools.

Individual tools can be selected by clicking in the Tools window. Tools can also be selected via key commands or MIDI commands.

Figure 3.19

The Tracks Window

The first tab in the Consolidated window is labeled Tracks. Press this tab to display the Tracks window. The Tracks window can also be opened from the Project menu, by using a key command, or by pressing a shortcut button. The default key command is Shift + T.

The Tracks window is an efficient place to set up and manage the session. Think of the Tracks window as the patchbay for Digital Performer. The Tracks window displays all the tracks in the sequence, including important functions such as track names and input and output assignments. The Tracks window provides for organization of tracks within folders, as well as assignment of track colors for at-a-glance identification.

The Tracks window is divided into a left and right side. There is a divider bar that separates those sides. Drag the divider bar left or right to show more or less of one side or the other.

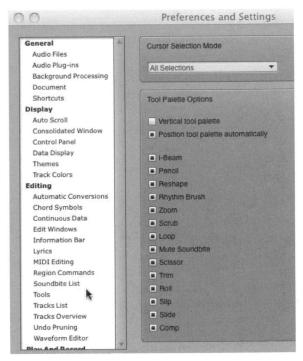

Figure 3.20

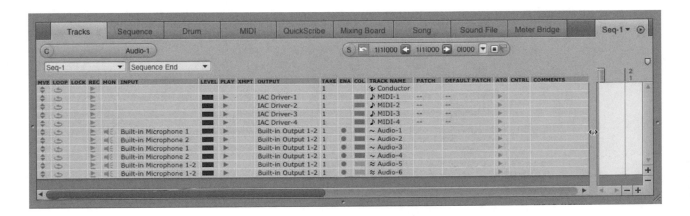

Figure 3.21

The right side of the window provides a general view of the contents of each track. When a new file is created, the right side of the Tracks window is empty, because no MIDI or audio has been recorded. As audio and MIDI is recorded into tracks, that data will be displayed on the right side of the Tracks window.

The left side of the Tracks Overview window displays a series of vertical columns. Each column describes an attribute of the track. To change the order of the columns, drag the column headers left or right. Column display can be customized by hiding or showing columns. Double-click on a column name or go to Preferences > Editing > Tracks List. Zoom the display of the Tracks window horizontally and vertically with the Plus and Minus buttons in the lower right-hand corner of the window.

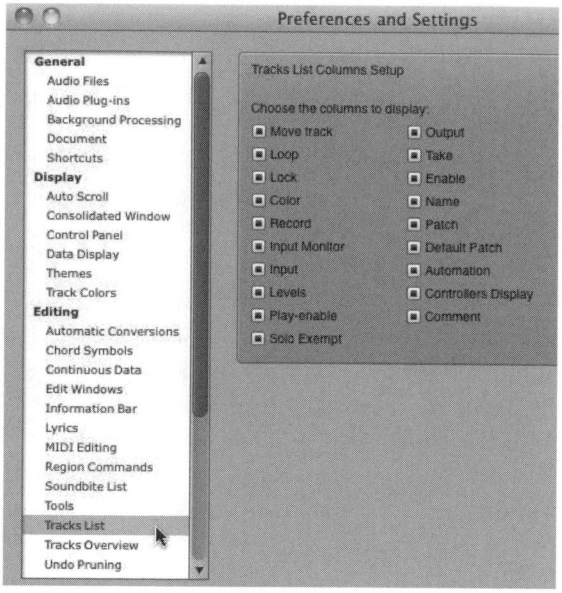

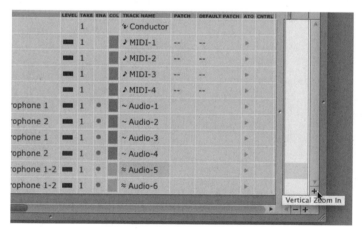

Figure 3.22

Naming Tracks

Before any recording is done, it is a good idea to name the tracks in the sequence. This is especially important for audio tracks. When Digital Performer records audio, it creates audio files. The names of these files are based on the track names. This means that if a track with the name of "Audio-1" records audio, the new file will be called "Audio-1." If the track is named "Bass Guitar," the newly created audio file will be called "Bass Guitar." It's much easier to keep track of and organize audio files when the file names reflect their recording sources.

Tracks can be renamed from any window that displays the track name. In the Tracks window, look for the Track Name column. Option-click or right-click on the track name to pop it up. Type in the new name.

Press the Enter key or the Up Arrow or Down Arrow to move to the next track for naming. Press the Return key to exit the naming mode.

Figure 3.23

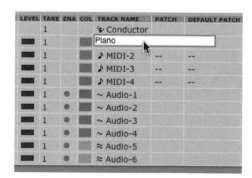

Figure 3.24

Track Types

Digital Performer uses different types of tracks for different types of data. MIDI is recorded into a MIDI track. A mono audio signal is recorded into a mono audio track. Stereo audio can be recorded into two mono audio tracks, or into a single stereo audio track. There are special types of tracks for virtual instruments called Instrument tracks. Digital Performer provides aux tracks and master fader tracks for audio routing. Every Digital Performer sequence also includes a Conductor track.

Look in the Track Name column. To the left of each track name is an icon. The icon describes the track type. An eighth-note icon means the track is a MIDI track. A single-wave icon means the track is a mono audio track. A double-wave icon means the track is a stereo audio track. An Instrument track is represented by a rectangle icon. An aux track is represented by a plug icon. A master fader track has a fader icon. The Conductor track is represented by an icon that looks like a stick figure holding a conductor's baton.

Figure 3.25

The Conductor Track

Regardless of whether it is used or not, every sequence in Digital Performer has a Conductor track. The Conductor track cannot be deleted from the sequence. The purpose of the Conductor track is to provide meter, key, and tempo changes. Track markers are also stored in the Conductor track. If there are no meter changes, key changes, tempo changes, or markers in the sequence, the Conductor track will be empty. If these events are embedded, the Conductor track will "conduct" the music.

Selecting Tracks

To select a track, click on its name field. The name field will become highlighted. Select multiple tracks by clicking-and-dragging up or down the Track Name column. Select noncontiguous tracks by holding down the Shift key and clicking on each track name.

Deleting Tracks

To delete a selected track or tracks, go to the Project menu and select Delete Tracks. Tracks can also be deleted by right-clicking anywhere in the Tracks window, or in the left edge of the Sequence Editor window.

Adding Tracks

To add a track, go to the Project menu and choose Add Track. This will display a submenu that lists different types of tracks. For example, if Add Track > MIDI Track is selected, a MIDI track will be added to the sequence. If no other tracks are selected when a new track is added, the new track will be added to the bottom of the track list. If any track is currently selected when a new track is added, the new track will appear immediately below the selected track.

It is also possible to add tracks by right-clicking anywhere in the Tracks window, or in the left edge of the Sequence Editor window.

Changing Track Order

To change the order of tracks in the Tracks window, use the handle in the MVE (Move) column to drag a track up or down in the Tracks window.

Folders

In a very large Digital Performer session, it is possible to end up with hundreds of tracks. Digital Performer provides a handy way to organize tracks using Folders. Select one or more tracks and go to Project > Track Folders > New Track Folder From Selected Tracks. The selected tracks will be moved into a folder.

Figure 3.26

Figure 3.27

Track folders can be named by Option-clicking on the folder name. Tracks can be dragged into an existing open track folder. It's even possible to nest folders inside of other folders, in order to organize large complex sequences. For example, there could be a folder called Orchestra that contains subfolders for the string section, woodwind section, and so on.

Track Colors

Digital Performer has the ability to assign colors to tracks. This is a useful tool for organization. For example, set the track colors for all the drum tracks to green, and all the vocal tracks to orange. This would make it very simple to tell the groups of tracks apart at a quick glance when looking at the Mixing Board window or Sequence Editor window. In the Tracks window, click on the COL column to change the color for a track. Select multiple tracks and choose Colors from the Setup menu. This will provide a range of options for changing the colors of the selected tracks. There are also additional track color options in Preferences > Display > Track Colors.

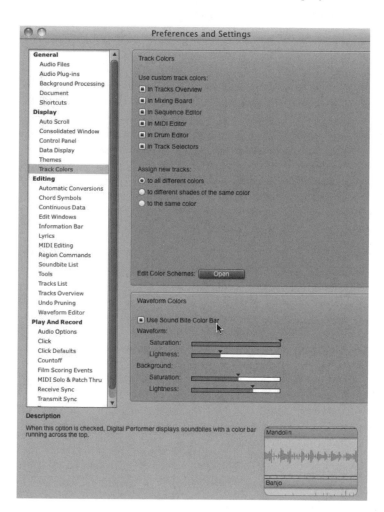

Figure 3.28

Themes

It is possible to change the colors, fonts, and many of the graphics in the Digital Performer interface. This can be done by changing Themes. Themes are preset configurations of colors and graphics within Digital Performer. Themes do not change the functionality of the program—they only change the look of the interface. Themes can be changed in Digital Performer Preferences > Display > Themes. Double-click on a theme preset to switch to that theme. There are also options to change VU meter and selection colors.

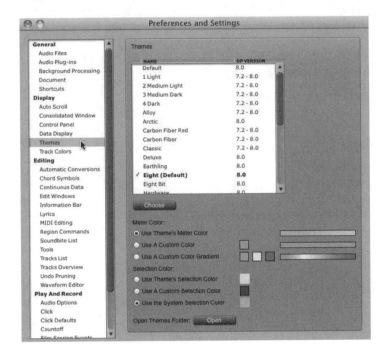

Figure 3.29

A theme can be changed at any time. A theme is not specific to a session file. A theme is a global configuration for all files opened within Digital Performer.

The Sequence Editor Window

The Sequence Editor window is where most audio and MIDI editing is done. Any combination of tracks in the sequence can be shown or hidden in the Sequence Editor window. The Sequence Editor window can zoom down to the sample level for a single audio track, or zoom out to show the entire contents of the sequence.

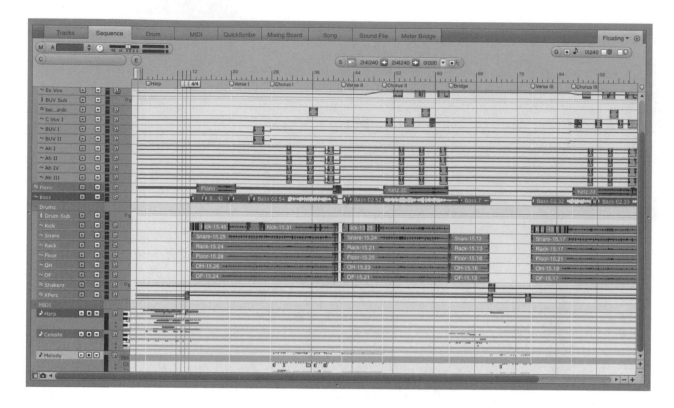

Figure 3.30

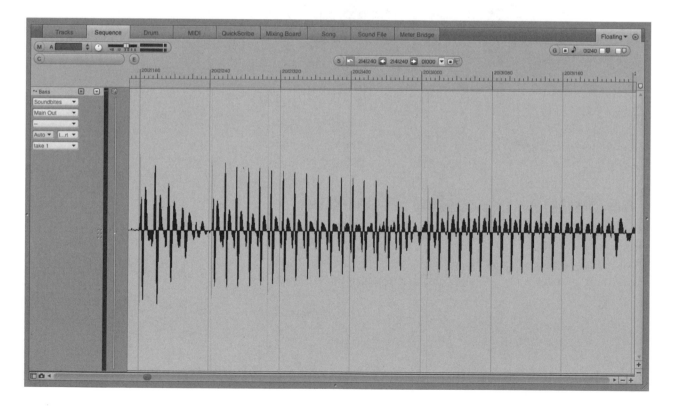

Figure 3.31

Markers

Markers are used to keep track of specific locations within the sequence. For example, markers can be used to label the verses and choruses of the song. They can also be used for locating the playback cursor in Digital Performer, which makes getting around inside the song very easy.

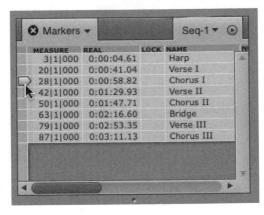

Open the Markers window from the Project menu. Initially, the window will be empty. Add a marker by choosing Add Marker from the minimenu in the upper left-hand corner. The marker will be added at the current sequence location.

Edit a marker name by Option-clicking on the name.

Change a marker location by clicking on the time filed on the left edge and entering a new time location.

Use markers to navigate within the sequence by clicking on the left edge of the Markers window.

Figure 3.32

The Mixing Board Window

Press the Mixing Board tab to open the Mixing Board window. Like the Sequence Editor window, tracks can be hidden or displayed in the Mixing Board window. The button to open the Track Selector window is in the bottom left-hand corner of the Mixing Board window.

The Mixing Board provides volume faders and pan controls for each track. The Mixing Board also provides input and output assignments, automation controls, mute, solo, and record buttons, sends, and inserts. It is also possible to display miniviews of dynamics and EQ plug-ins in the audio fader strips.

Figure 3.33

The purpose of the Mixing Board is to set up the volume and pan balance of the tracks in the sequence. The Mixing Board is where plug-in effects for audio and MIDI tracks are inserted. The Mixing Board also provides sends for additional audio track mixes.

There are two basic ways to automate a mix in Digital Performer. Automation data can be manually inserted into a track in an edit window. The other technique for automation to is play the sequence, and move faders, panners, effects, and parameters and record those moves as live automation. This type of automation is done from the Mixing Board.

The VU meters next to the tracks faders display track output volume during playback. To check audio input volume for recording, use the Audio Monitor window.

The Audio Monitor

The Audio Monitor window can be opened from the Studio menu or from a sidebar. The Audio Monitor displays audio signal level as it comes into Digital Performer. The purpose of the Audio Monitor window is to check signal level before any signal is recorded. It is also possible to set a new destination for audio file recording from the Audio Monitor window.

When an audio track is record-enabled, a VU meter in the Audio Monitor window will be highlighted. There is a clip indicator to the right of the VU meter. When signal is present at the assigned input of the audio track, activity will be visible in the highlighted VU meter. This level cannot be adjusted from inside Digital Performer. Set the record level from the audio interface, or by changing the volume of the input device. It is desirable to see solid signal without clipping. If the clip indicator does light up, turn down the input volume. To clear the clip indicator, press Command + / (backslash) on the keyboard (or choose Clear All Clip Indicators from the Studio menu).

To the right of the clip indicator is the name of the file that will be created when audio is recorded. This file name is initially based on the track name. Change how audio file naming works by choosing options from the Audio Monitor window minimenu.

To the right of the file name is a column that shows how much time can be recorded into the armed track, based on available hard drive space. Clicking on this field will toggle to display available time or available disk space.

To the right of the Available Time column is the Take Folder column. This displays a path to where the audio file will be recorded. By default, audio files are recorded into an Audio Files folder, which is created inside the project folder.

The take file destination can be changed. To record the take files to a location other than the Audio Files folder in the project folder, double-click on the file name in the Audio Monitor window. A window will open that allows a new location to be selected for the next file that is recorded by this track. Choose any location on any hard drive that is connected to the computer.

Chunks

Digital Performer can have multiple independent sequences inside a single session file. A sequence inside a Digital Performer session file is called a "chunk."

The Chunks Window

A new Digital Performer session file includes one sequence chunk. By default this initial sequence is called Seq-1.

The Chunks window can be opened via shortcut button or key command, from the Sidebar window, or from the Studio menu. The default key command to open the Chunks window is Shift + C. Sequence chunks can be renamed by Option-clicking in the name field in the Chunks window.

Only one sequence chunk can be play-enabled at a time. The blue Play button in the Chunks window indicates the currently active sequence chunk. Any windows in the Consolidated window that are specific to the current sequence chunk will update when a different chunk is play-enabled.

Multiple Versions of a Sequence

The Chunks window allows the composer to have multiple versions of

Figure 3.34

the same sequence within a single session file. A sequence can be duplicated. The duplicated sequence can then be edited without affecting the original version. To duplicate a sequence, select the sequence in the Chunks window and choose Duplicate Sequence from the minimenu.

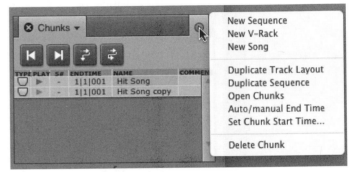

The Set List

The Chunks window can act as a set list for live performance. Each sequence chunk can represent a separate song in the set list. Sequence chunks can be play-enabled remotely via MIDI messages. This is set up in the Commands window.

Figure 3.35

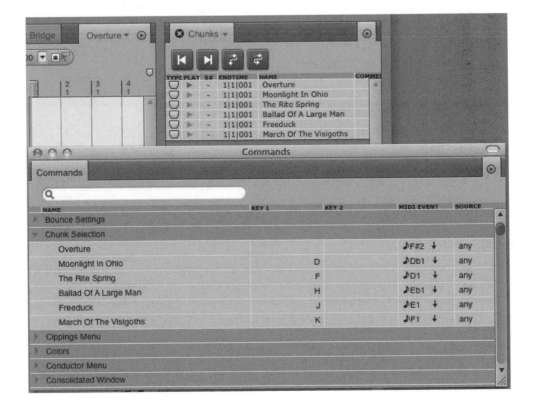

Figure 3.36

The Album Project

Sequence chunks can be used to represent separate songs in a CD or album project. There can be multiple versions of songs represented as separate chunks. A specific sequence chunk can be created to prepare for stereo mastering and final CD output.

Film Cues

When working on a movie or TV show soundtrack, there are usually multiple pieces of music in the soundtrack that are called *cues*. Separate sequence chunks can be created for each cue within the soundtrack. These sequence chunks can then be arranged along a single timeline that represents the entire movie or TV show. This is set up in the Song window.

Creating New Sequences

The minimenu in the Chunks window provides options to create a new, empty sequence chunk, to duplicate an existing sequence chunk, or to create a new sequence chunk based on the track layout of an existing sequence.

It is also possible to create a new sequence chunk based on a selection made in the Tracks window. This can be useful to cut up an existing sequence into smaller sequences. For example, an ensemble may record multiple takes one after another into a single sequence. Later, it may be desirable to separate each take into a separate sequence. To make a new sequence chunk from a selection in an existing sequence, make the selection in the Tracks window, then go to the menu in the upper left-hand corner and choose Copy Selection To New Sequence.

Figure 3.37

Combining Sequences

It is possible to combine separate sequences into a single sequence. To do this, play-enable the first sequence and open its Tracks window. Open the Chunks window. Drag the chunk icon from the left of the second sequence in the Chunks window to the left side of the Tracks window of the first sequence. The left side of the Tracks window will be highlighted. Release the mouse button, and the second sequence will be imported into the first sequence.

V-Racks

V-Racks are a specific type of chunk. A V-Rack does not contain any sequence. A V-Rack can contain instrument tracks, aux tracks, and master fader tracks. To create a V-Rack, choose New V-Rack from the Chunks window minimenu. Double-click on the name of the V-Rack in the Chunks window to open the V-Rack. V-Racks open in the Mixing Board window.

Use Add Track from the Project menu to add instrument, aux, or master fader tracks. Set the input and output assignments for these tracks at the bottom of each fader strip in the mixing board. Inputs for instrument tracks are available as outputs to any MIDI track in any play-enabled sequence chunk.

V-Racks allow a common set of virtual instruments and effects to be available to multiple sequence chunks. This means that when switching between sequence chunks, Digital Performer does not need to unload one set of instruments and effects and then reload another set.

Songs

In Digital Performer terminology, a Song is a collection of sequence chunks that are placed on a single timeline. When the Song is played, each separate sequence will play at its specified start time.

The Song window can be opened from a tab in the Consolidated window, or by adding a New Song via the Chunks window minimenu.

Cue Chunks and Chain Chunks Modes

There are four buttons at the top of the Chunks window. The two buttons on the left change which sequence chunk is currently play-enabled. They will cue the previous or next sequence chunk in the list below.

The third button from the left is the Cue Chunks button. When this button is engaged, a sequence chunk will play until its programmed end time, and then the next sequence chunk in the list will be play-enabled.

The button on the right is the Chain Chunks button. When this button is engaged, the Chunks window is in Medley mode. Each chunk will play until its programmed end time, and then the next sequence chunk will be enabled and automatically played. Sequence chunk end times can be programmed by selecting the sequence chunk and choosing Auto/Manual End Time from the Chunks window minimenu.

The Cue Chunks buttons can all be remotely controlled via MIDI messages or computer keyboard commands.

Undo History

Digital Performer keeps track of each edit that is made in the session. Under the Edit menu is the Undo command. The default key command for undo is Command + Z.

There is also a window available under the Edit menu called Undo History. The Undo History window shows a list of all edits. Each edit has a basic description, and the date and time it was made.

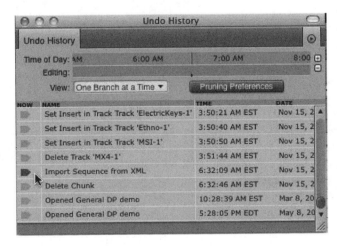

It is possible to step back through every edit made from the time the session was created. By clicking on a specific event in the Undo History window, Digital Performer will jump to that edit point.

The Undo History keeps track of all edits, including edits that have been undone. These are called Edit Branches and are displayed and available for recall in the Undo History window.

Figure 3.38

If undo events involve changing a sound file, a copy of the sound file is created. This copy is stored in a folder in the project folder called Undo History. Depending on the type of editing done in Digital Performer, it is possible that many sound files will end up in the Undo History folder. This can take up significant amounts of hard drive space. Therefore, Digital Performer provides a way to manage the undo history. In the upper right-hand corner of the Undo History window is a minimenu with Undo Pruning Preferences.

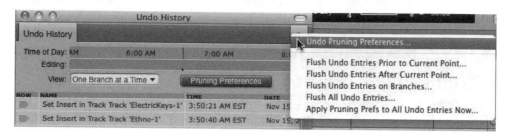

Figure 3.39

The Soundbites Window

The Soundbites window contains a list of every soundbite that is currently being referenced by the Digital Performer session file. This includes all soundbites that are being used in sequence tracks, and can also include soundbites that are not currently being used in any track in the session.

The Soundbites window can be opened from the Project menu or in a sidebar window. The Soundbites window can be opened with a shortcut, a MIDI remote command, or a key command. The default key command to open the Soundbites window is Shift + B. The Soundbites window displays a list of every soundbite that is currently referenced by the session file.

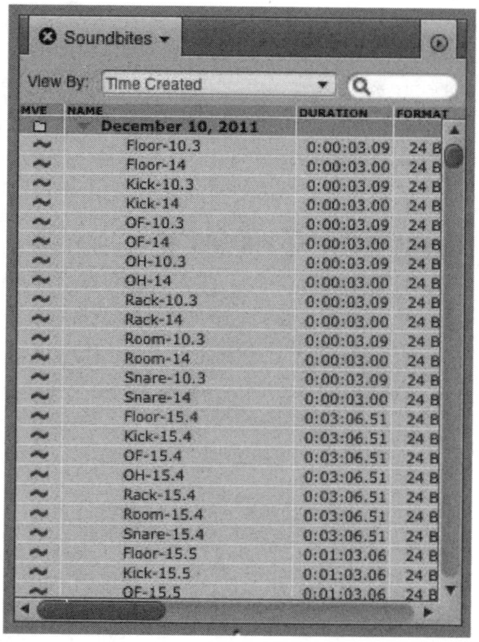

The Soundbites window has a series of columns that display information about each soundbite. These columns include

Figure 3.40

the soundbite name, duration, creation time, and sound-file name. Double-clicking on the top of any column will open the Soundbite List Columns Setup window in the Digital Performer Preferences.

A soundbite is a region inside a digital audio sound file. Therefore, it is possible to have multiple soundbites that are all referencing the same sound file.

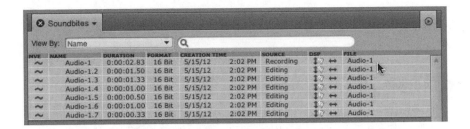

Figure 3.41

It is possible to search for soundbites by name. Soundbites can also be sorted in different ways with the View By pop-up menu.

It is possible for a session to reference soundbites that are not currently being used in any sequence tracks. In some cases it may be desirable to delete these unused soundbites and their parent sound files. Go the Soundbites window minimenu and choose Select Unused Soundbites. All soundbites that are not currently being used in an audio track in any sequence in the current session will be selected. Now go back to the minimenu and choose either Remove From List or Delete. Remove From List will remove the references of the selected soundbites and sound files from the Digital Performer session, but will not delete the soundbites and sound files from the hard drive. Delete will remove the selected soundbite references from the Digital Performer session, and will delete the sound files from the hard drive. This can be an effective way of cleaning up unused takes and edits.

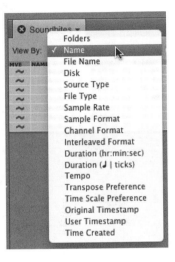

Figure 3.42

The Bundles Window

Digital Performer uses bundles to manage audio and MIDI signal flow in, out, and through the software. Open the Bundles window from the Studio menu or shortcut button. The Bundles window can be opened via remote MIDI command or key command. The default key command to open the Bundles window is Shift + U.

A bundle is an audio or MIDI channel or group of channels. The Bundles window has tabs to display audio inputs and outputs, audio buses, virtual instrument sends and auxiliary outputs, and external MIDI devices.

Audio input and output bundles provide access to the audio interface hardware that is currently configured. Input and output bundles can be mono, stereo, or multichannel for surround sound.

Bus bundles are used for internal routing of audio signals within Digital Performer. Bus bundles can also be in mono, stereo, or multichannel.

Instrument buses represent the secondary outputs of currently loaded virtual instruments. Not all virtual instruments have sends or auxiliary outputs. If the instrument does feature secondary audio outputs, they will automatically be listed in the Bundles window.

It is possible to create new input, output, bus, and MIDI device bundles directly in the Bundles window. It is also possible to create new audio input, output, and bus bundles in other windows where audio inputs and outputs can be assigned. For example, clicking on the Input column for an audio track in the Tracks window provides the option to create a new input bundle.

It is possible to name bundles by Option-clicking in the Name column. This is useful for naming interface input and output assignments. It is also helpful to name buses when they are used as effects sends or subgroups.

Importing Audio and MIDI

Audio and MIDI data can be recorded into tracks in Digital Performer. It is also possible to import different types of existing data into a Digital Performer session file.

Importing Audio

Audio files can be dragged directly into Digital Performer. Audio can be dragged from the computer desktop into the Soundbites window. Audio can be dragged from the Soundbites window or the computer desktop into sequence tracks. Mono audio must be dragged to a mono track. Stereo audio must be dragged into a stereo audio track.

It is also possible to drag audio files into the left side of the Tracks window. This will cause Digital Performer to make new audio tracks for each soundbite that is included in the drag. This feature is very useful when importing multiple audio files from a different sequencer application into a DP session.

Importing MIDI

The most common standard format for MIDI information is Standard MIDI File. Standard MIDI Files can be dragged into the Chunks window to create a new sequence chunk. Standard MIDI Files can be dragged into the left side of the Tracks window of an existing sequence. This will import the MIDI tracks in the file into that sequence.

Loading from Other Digital Performer Session Files

It is possible to import the contents of Digital Performer session files into other Digital Performer session files. This can include all sequence chunks, soundbites, bundles, and other information associated with the session.

Inside a current Digital Performer session file, go to the File menu and choose Load. A window will open that allows a second Digital Performer session file to be selected. Select the second Digital Performer session file and choose Open. A Load dialog box will appear. This is where the sequences and other options are selected to be imported.

Select the desired sequences and options and press OK. The newly loaded sequences will appear in the Chunks window.

It is also possible to load one sequence into another by dragging a closed Digital Performer session file into the Chunks window of an open Digital Performer session file. This will cause the Load dialog box to open, providing all the load options.

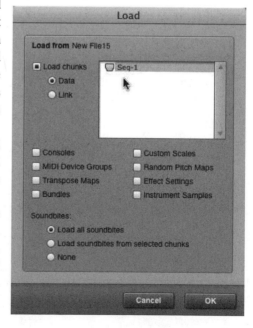

Figure 3.43

Notation

Digital Performer can display MIDI notes as sheet music notation. MIDI tracks can be displayed as staves. Any combination of MIDI tracks can be displayed, allowing the creation of individual parts, full scores, and lead sheets.

The notation functions of Digital Performer include text and musical markings such as dynamics symbols and arrangement symbols. Pages can be formatted and printed or saved as PDF files.

Navigating the QuickScribe Window

Open the QuickScribe window via a tab in the Consolidated window or a shortcut button. The QuickScribe window can also be opened from the Project menu, through remote MIDI command, or by key command. The default key command to open the QuickScribe window is Shift + Q. To open the QuickScribe window, there must be at least one MIDI track in the sequence.

The QuickScribe window displays a page that is based on the print driver settings. Change print driver settings by going to the File menu and choosing Page Setup. The paper size that is selected in the Page Setup window is what is displayed in the QuickScribe window.

The QuickScribe window uses the Track Selector to show or hide MIDI tracks. MIDI tracks are displayed as staves on the QuickScribe window page. The order that the staves appear in is based on the order of the MIDI tracks in the Tracks window or Sequence Editor window. Changing the track order in the Tracks window or Sequence Editor window will change the order of the staves in the QuickScribe window.

Working with Staves

Digital Performer will display staves with clef markings based on the range of notes in the MIDI track. To change a clef for a stave, go to the QuickScribe window minimenu and select Options > Track Options. Initially, the Track Options window displays global settings for staves. To change the clef settings for individual tracks, click on the pop-up menu at the top of the window and select the track to be changed. Uncheck the Use Default button to display options. Now choose the clef for the selected track, as well as other track-specific options.

If a grand staff is selected for a MIDI track, Digital Performer will use an internal transcription engine to intelligently assign notes to the treble and bass clef staves. To switch a note or group of notes to the other stave, select those notes and choose Switch Staff from the QuickScribe window minimenu.

Staves can be transposed for display only. This is helpful if the sheet music is to be played by transposing instruments such as trumpet or clarinet.

Meter and Key Signature

The default key of a new sequence in Digital Performer is C major. To change a key signature, go to Project > Conductor Track > Change Key. Key signatures can be changed at any point in the sequence. The key signature will be displayed in sharps and flats on the staff in the QuickScribe window.

By default, a new sequence in Digital Performer has a meter of 4/4 time. To change meter, go to Project > Conductor Track > Change Meter.

It is possible to change meter and key signature directly in the QuickScribe window. Click on an existing key signature or meter marking to get the menu that allows changing the key or meter at that point in the sequence.

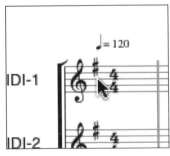

Figure 3.43.1

Note Entry

The QuickScribe window displays all MIDI notes in a track as notation. MIDI can be recorded into a track while the QuickScribe window is open. This includes using the Step Record function. It is also possible to enter notes in the QuickScribe window by clicking directly on the staff with the mouse.

The Tool palette can be shown or hidden via the QuickScribe window minimenu. The Tool palette includes selections for different note durations. Select a note value and click on a staff. That will enter the note into the track and display it on the staff. The Commands window includes a list of note values and their key assignments. By using key commands to change note values on the fly, it is possible to create a score by "drawing the dots on the paper."

Transcription and Note Spelling

MIDI does not describe a note name. Each MIDI note is represented as a number. For example, MIDI does not describe whether a note is a C<#> or D. When MIDI notes are displayed as notation in Digital Performer, the software must transcribe the MIDI note information into notes on a staff. Transcription includes note spelling, as well as note duration.

Digital Performer displays note spelling based on key signature. It is possible to override the transcription engine and change the spelling of a note. In the QuickScribe Tool palette, select the Note Speller tool. Click on a note and a menu will open showing alternate spelling choices for the selected note.

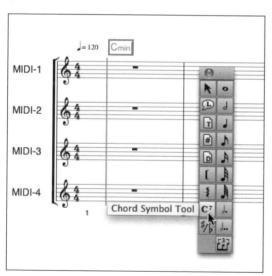

Figure 3.44

Digital Performer displays rests based on the note content within each bar. Rests are displayed based on note values and the meter of the sequence.

The duration of a MIDI note is used to determine its rhythmic display in the QuickScribe window. To change the duration value of the note in the QuickScribe window, select the correct duration from the Tool palette and click on the note to change it.

Chords

Chord changes can be displayed as text. There is a specific tool to use to display chord changes in the QuickScribe window. Select the Chord Symbol tool and click on the QuickScribe page to create a text box. Enter a chord as text into the box. Press Return to exit the chord-naming mode.

Chord symbols will follow transpositions within the sequence. Select the chord symbols in the QuickScribe window and choose Transpose from the Region menu. Choose the transposition options and check the Transpose Chord Symbols box.

Lyrics and Text

Several different tools can be used to enter text onto QuickScribe pages. The QuickScribe Tool palette has separate tools for entering page text, page numbering, and the date. There are many ways you can display text on the page. Any fonts available to the OS can be used.

Lyrics are words that are connected to MIDI notes. There is a separate window in which to enter lyrics. Open the Lyrics window either as a sidebar window, or from the Project menu. The Lyrics window is a simple word processor. Text can be typed in. Text can also be copied and pasted from other software programs into the Lyrics window.

Once words have been entered into the Lyrics window, they can be flowed to a MIDI track and assigned to specific MIDI notes. Display the MIDI track that describes the melody of the song. Double-click on the staff right before the first note where a lyric is to be assigned. This will locate the sequence cursor to that point. Select the lyrics to be assigned to the MIDI notes. Press the Auto Flow button. The selected lyrics will be assigned to the MIDI notes.

Figure 3.45

Lyrics can be further edited on the QuickScribe page. For example, double-click on a lyric to pop it up for editing. Insert a hyphen and the word will be extended to the next MIDI note, pushing all the following lyrics to the appropriate spot to accommodate the change.

Figure 3.46

Click on a word within the lyric to select it, and use the Left and Right Arrow keys to nudge the word on the page.

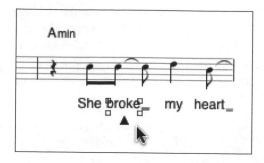

Figure 3.47

Dynamics Markings

From the QuickScribe window minimenu select the Dynamics palette. Select a dynamics marking and click on the QuickScribe page to enter. Crescendo and decrescendo markings can be dragged to fit over the desired notes.

Dynamics marking do not change MIDI volume or velocity on playback. Dynamics markings are display only.

Arranging for Lead Sheets

The QuickScribe window has many options for creating lead sheets. From the QuickScribe window minimenu, open the Arrangement palette. Select any arrangement marking and click on the QuickScribe page to enter.

Multiple bars containing no notes can be displayed as a single bar with a consolidated rest symbol. Notes can be designated for display only or for playback only with no display on the QuickScribe page.

Bars can be hidden inside other bars. This technique is used for repeating verses and choruses. These and other arrangement options are all available under the QuickScribe window minimenu.

Printing

What you see in the QuickScribe window is what will be printed. The QuickScribe window will print to any printer connected to the computer.

The print window also includes an option to save to a PDF file. The PDF file can then be sent as an e-mail attachment, displayed on the Internet, or printed from any computer.

Chapter 4
RECORDING

There are two ways to get audio or MIDI data into a track in Digital Performer. Data can be imported into a track, and data can be recorded into a track. This chapter describes recording techniques, including transport controls, working with record and playback loops, overdubbing, and punching.

Click and tempo maps can be an important part of composition and recording. Digital Performer provides all the tools required to set up and control click tracks and tempos within the sequence. This chapter will also describe how to work with click tracks and tempo changes in Digital Performer.

The Control Panel

The Control Panel contains the basic functions for controlling record and playback in Digital Performer. The Control Panel can contain additional functions such as the Tool palate and Shortcut buttons. The Control Panel is customizable in terms of what is displayed. The Control Panel can be a stand-alone window, or it can be integrated into the Consolidated window.

Transport

In the Control Panel, there are transport buttons. These buttons and other functions control the play, record, and current timeline location of the Digital Performer sequence. To show the current record or playback location in the sequence, Digital Performer uses two counters and a playback wiper. The counters are displayed in the Control Panel window, and can also be displayed in a separate Counter window. The playback wiper is visible in the graphic editing windows. When Digital Performer is in playback or record mode, the counters change to reflect the current timeline location, and the playback wiper scrolls across all graphic editing windows.

The main transport buttons are, from left to right: Fast Rewind, Slow Rewind, Slow Forward, Return To Zero, Stop, Play, Pause, and Record. These buttons are linked to keyboard shortcuts, and they can also be controlled via external MIDI messages.

Check the Commands window under the Setup menu for keyboard shortcuts and MIDI remote commands.

Below the main transport buttons are a series of transport-related functions. These buttons engage the following functions: Auto Rewind, Auto Stop, Memory Cycle, Link Playback To Memory, Link Selection To Memory, Auto Record, Overdub, Count-off, Wait For Note, and Slave To External Sync.

Counter and Time Display

Figure 4.1

The Counter provides a numeric display of the current location within the timeline of the sequence. There are two Counters in the Control Panel, which can be set to show two different time formats simultaneously.

Figure 4.2

Figure 4.3

There is also a dedicated Counter window, which can be customized and resized. Open the Counter window from the Studio menu or as a sidebar window. The Counter window can be opened with a shortcut button or remote command. The default key command to open the Counter window is Shift + J.

The counters can also display markers If there are any markers in the Markers window, the current marker can be displayed in the Counter window. This can be helpful for providing a quick reference to the current sequence location as described by text. In this picture, the Markers window and the Counter window are displayed in a sidebar of the Consolidated window.

Time Format Display

The Digital Performer sequence timeline can be measured with different time formats. Time formats display as a ruler in graphic edit windows. Sequence events are assigned to locations on the timeline. Time can be viewed in multiple formats.

It is possible to make global changes to how time is displayed in Digital Performer. Under the Setup menu is the Time Formats window.

This window contains many options for customizing how time is displayed in Digital Performer.

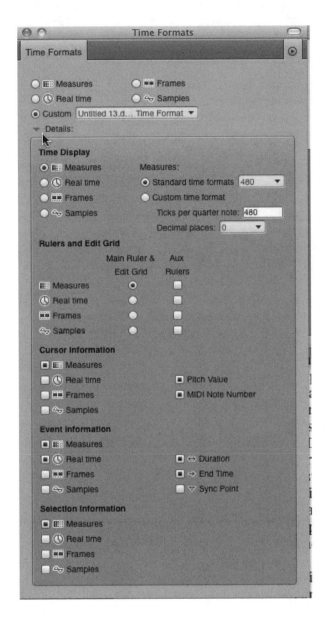

Figure 4.4

In addition to the counters, current sequence timeline location is also displayed in the ruler of any graphic editing window with the playback wiper. The playback wiper is a vertical line that represents the current play location.

A timeline ruler may display multiple time formats, depending on the current settings in the Time Formats window.

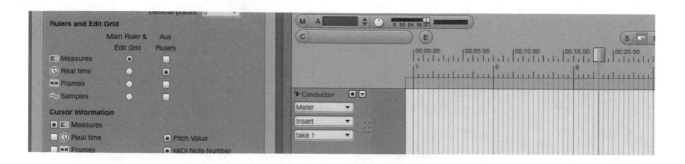

Figure 4.5

Time can be displayed in bars, beats, and ticks. Bar lines are based on a tempo map within the sequence. The number of beats within a bar is determined by the meter that is assigned in the Conductor track. Ticks are divisions of beats. The default resolution of Digital Performer is 480 ticks per beat. That resolution can be changed in the Time Formats window under the Setup menu.

The sequence timeline can be viewed in Real Time format. The real-time display will show elapsed minutes and seconds within the sequence timeline.

Time can be viewed as SMPTE frame time. SMPTE frame time is typically used when Digital Performer is used to compose sound for picture. SMPTE frame time is based on film frame location, and is used to describe position within film or video.

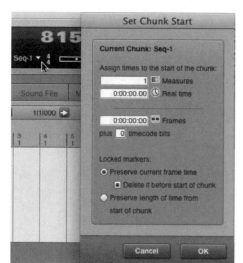

Figure 4.6

SMPTE frame time is used to synchronize a Digital Performer sequence to video. For example, music may not start exactly at the beginning of a movie. If music starts, for example, one minute into the movie, then that means the SMPTE start time of the sequence should be set to one minute. However, the music still starts at bar 1, so the composer needs to be able to offset the first bar number of the sequence to the correct SMPTE frame time within the sequence. This is done in the Set Chunk Start Time window. Set Chunk Start is available from the menu in either the Control Panel window or the Chunks window minimenu.

When working with SMPTE frame time, there are different frame rates that may be used in the video. The frame rate of Digital Performer should match the frame rate of the video file. Set the frame rate for the current sequence from the pop-up menu in the Control Panel window.

Time can be viewed in numbers of samples. These will be very large numbers, and the numbering will depend on the sample rate of the audio hardware. For example, if the sample rate is set to 44.1 kHz and the transport of Digital Performer is set to exactly one second, the Sample Counter will read 44,100.

Locating

It is important to be able to locate to any point on the sequence timeline instantly. There are many ways to change the current record or playback location in Digital Performer.

Wherever the playback wiper is visible, the wiper can be moved by clicking-and-dragging the wiper with the mouse. In

Figure 4.7

the various graphic editing windows in Digital Performer, there is a ruler at the top of each window that displays the current position in the timeline. Double-click in that ruler, and the playback wiper will jump to that location.

Click on a field in one of the counters in the Control Panel window. The field will become highlighted. Enter a new number and press the Enter key. Digital Performer will reposition the current location to the location that was typed in. The default keyboard shortcut to enter a new counter location is the decimal key on the numeric keypad. If markers are displayed in a counter, clicking on the marker will display a list of all markers in the sequence, and any marker location can be selected.

The Markers window can also be used to locate within a sequence. Click on the left edge of the Markers window to locate to that marker position.

Start and Stop Times

Start and stop times are locations on the timeline that are used for auto-rewind, auto-stop, and loop points. The start and stop times are displayed in the Control Panel window, under the counter.

There are several ways to enter a location into the Start and Stop fields. Click on the word "Start" or "Stop," and the current counter location will be entered into that field. This operation can also be done with a remote keyboard or MIDI command.

Click to highlight a number in the Start or Stop field. Enter a new number. Use the Tab key to advance to the next edit field. Press Enter to exit the edit mode.

Figure 4.8

When a transport function button that uses a remembered start or stop time is engaged, an icon is displayed in the time ruler of most edit windows. The location of the Start or Stop icon can be changed by dragging left or right in those windows.

To the right of the start and stop times is an arrow that opens a menu. The menu allows start and stop times to be entered, remembered, and recalled. Saved start and stop times can be helpful when playback loops are used in live performance.

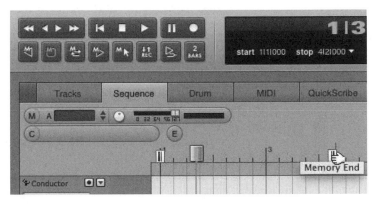

Figure 4.9

Auto Rewind and Auto Stop

The first transport function button is the Auto Rewind button. If Auto Rewind is engaged, the Return To Zero button changes to Return To Memory Location. When the Return To Memory Location button is pressed, the playback wiper will locate to the currently entered start time. The memory return location is set in the Start field.

The next transport function button is Auto Stop. Auto Stop allows a time to be preset when the sequence playback will automatically stop. Also, when Auto Stop is engaged, the playback wiper will go to the currently entered start time when the Return To Zero is pressed. The stop time is entered to the right of the start time.

If both the Auto Rewind and Auto Stop buttons are engaged, pressing Stop in the main transport controls will automatically return the playback wiper to the start time.

Memory Cycle/Playback/Record Loop

The Memory Cycle button engages a playback loop in Digital Performer. When the Memory Cycle button is engaged, the transport will loop inside the start and stop time. The Memory Cycle can be engaged or disengaged during record or playback. Memory Cycle can be controlled with keyboard or remote MIDI commands.

Record mode can be engaged or disengaged at any time during memory cycle playback. How Digital Performer handles recording of MIDI and audio during Memory Cycle mode is determined by the Overdub mode.

In the studio, memory cycle is useful for setting up a playback or record loop. It is possible to mix, overdub, and edit while a looped section of the sequence plays.

Memory cycle can also be a powerful tool for live performance. Memory cycle can be used to vamp within a section of a sequence. The memory cycle loop can be engaged or disengaged on the fly, and it is possible to change the loop location during playback for vamping over different sections of the sequence.

Recording Audio and MIDI

Digital Performer records audio and MIDI data into tracks. Audio records to an audio track. MIDI records to a MIDI track. The following section describes how to set up and record audio and MIDI into tracks in Digital Performer.

Arming Tracks

To record into an audio or MIDI track in Digital Performer, the track must be record-armed. Record-arm the track in the Tracks window, Mixing Board window, or other edit windows.

The Record Button

Once a track is record-armed, put Digital Performer into Record mode by pressing the Record button in the Control Panel. The Record button can be engaged with a mouse-click, keyboard command, or remote MIDI command. The default key command for record is the 3 key on the numeric keypad.

Punching

It is possible to press the Record button while Digital Performer is in Play mode. This allows Digital Performer to punch-in to Record mode on the fly. If the Record button is pressed a second time while Digital Performer is in Play mode, the track (or multiple tracks) will go out of Record mode. Punching in and out can be controlled via mouse-click, keyboard shortcut, or remote MIDI command.

Punch-in and -out points can be automated. Press the Auto-Record button to engage automatic punch-in and punch-out. When Auto-Record is engaged, In and Out Times are displayed under the counter. Punch-in and -out times are also displayed in graphic editing windows as icons in the timeline.

Figure 4.10

Digital Performer has a feature called Punch Guard. Punch Guard records audio before and after a punch-in. This means that if the punch-in is late, or if Digital Performer is taken out of Record mode too early, the missed audio is preserved. After the record pass, it is possible to edge-edit the audio to reveal audio before and after the punch-in or punch-out points.

Overdubbing

The Overdub button is under the main transport buttons in the Control Panel. Overdub can also be engaged or disengaged with keyboard shortcuts and remote MIDI commands. The default key command to engage Overdub mode is the * (star) key in the numeric keypad.

When the Overdub button is engaged, recording into a MIDI track will leave any existing MIDI in the track undisturbed at the record location. If overdub is not engaged when recording into a MIDI track, any existing MIDI in the track at the record location will be deleted, and then replaced with the new MIDI data.

Figure 4.11

When recording into an audio track, if the Overdub button is engaged, a new audio file will be recorded on top of any current audio file in the track. The original audio file will be underneath the new audio file. If overdub is not engaged, existing audio in the track will be replaced by the newly recorded audio.

Takes

It is possible to have multiple takes within any track in a sequence. Takes allow multiple versions of the contents of a track to be recorded, recalled, and edited.

Track takes can be added or deleted at any time. Takes can be named. Takes can be expanded to separate tracks. Separate tracks can be consolidated into a single track as multiple takes.

Track takes can be controlled via remote MIDI or computer key commands. Track take options can also be accessed from the Tracks window and the Sequence window.

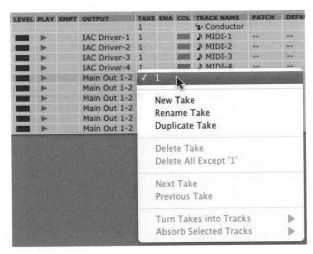

As new takes are created in a track, one take will always be the currently enabled take. Choose the currently enabled take from the Takes column. It is possible to create a new take and copy data from other takes into the new take to create a comp take.

- Make a time-range selection within a track.
- Copy the current selection.
- Change the currently enabled take.
- Choose the Paste command.
- The selected data will be pasted into the selected time range.

Figure 4.12

Click Tracks

A click track is a metronomic signal that is used to provide a tempo reference within a sequence or musical composition. Digital Performer provides sophisticated functions to create click tracks.

Click

Digital Performer can provide a click track. The click will follow the tempo of the sequence. The click can trigger an audio sound, a MIDI event, or a video flash. The click can be a simple quarter-note click, or it can be a sophisticated click pattern. Click tracks can be programmed to change patterns and click resolutions, and even to turn the click on and off. By default, Digital Performer provides a simple quarter-note click, and provides separate settings for downbeat and nondownbeat click sounds.

Click and Count-Off Options

The Click button is in the upper right-hand corner of the Control Panel. In the Click and Count-off window, there are settings for video, MIDI, and audio click. There are settings for when the click will sound. There are settings for click count-offs. Double-click on the Click button to open the Click Options window.

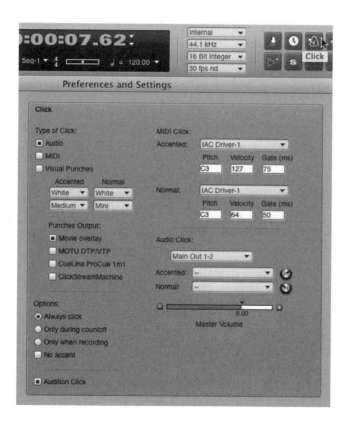

Figure 4.13

Audio Click

Digital Performer can generate a click as an audio signal. That audio signal can be directly routed to the outputs of your audio monitor system. In the Click and Count-off Options window, there is an assignment for the output destination of the audio click.

There are also pop-up menus to assign the audio click sounds. If the output assignment or audio click assignment is displayed in italics, then that means the output destination or sound must be reassigned.

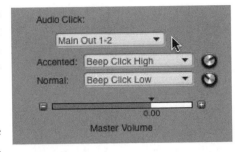

MIDI Click

Digital Performer can generate a MIDI note and send that as a click to a MIDI output. If there is a virtual instrument or hardware MIDI module that can make some sort of a click sound, the MIDI can be routed to that device.

Figure 4.14

Video Click

If Digital Performer is playing back a movie, a video click can be superimposed onto the movie. The size and color of the video click can be specified in the Click Preferences window.

Options

Different click behaviors are available. For example, to hear the click only when recording, or only during count-off, set these options in the Click Preferences window.

Count-Off and Click Patterns

It is possible to program Digital Performer to count off before engaging in record or playback. The Count-off button is located below the main transport buttons.

Double-click on the Count-off button to open the Count-off options in the Preferences window. The count-off time can be programmed, as can whether count-off will only happen when Digital Performer is in Record mode.

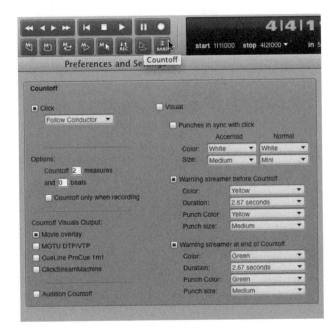

Figure 4.15

In addition to setting count-off options in this window, it is also possible to program Digital Performer to use a click pattern instead of a standard click. The click can also be programmed to follow custom changes that are entered into the Conductor track. Choose a saved click pattern from the pop-up menu in the Count-off Options window.

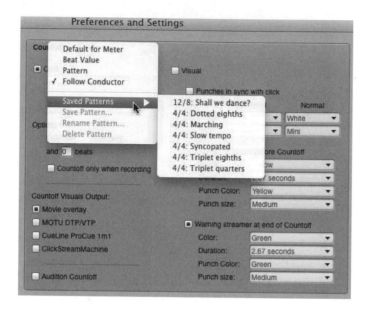

Figure 4.16

Click patterns can be programmed under Click Defaults in the Preferences window.

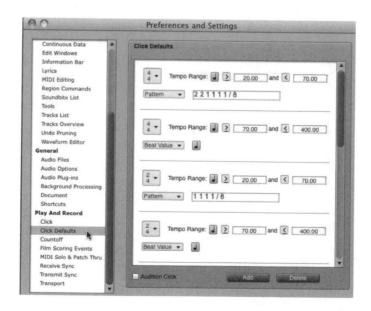

Figure 4.17

Printing the Click to an Audio Track

To create an audio click track in Digital Performer, the click can be recorded into an audio track. For the Audio Click output, choose New Mono Bundle > Bus 1 from the pop-up menu. If audio Bus 1 is already in use somewhere else in the mix, choose a different, unused bus.

Create a mono audio track. Set the input of the track to bus 1, or whatever bus is assigned for the Audio Click output. Name the audio track. Record-arm the track. Engage the Click button. Press Record in the Control Panel. Digital Performer will play the click and will record it as an audio file into the audio track.

Working with Tempo and Meter

Digital Performer provides powerful tools for creating tempo maps. Additionally, Digital Performer provides a time ruler based on bars and beats that is referenced to the tempo map. It is possible to program tempo and meter changes into a Digital Performer sequence.

Tempo Within a Sequence

A Digital Performer sequence can have an implied beats-per-minute tempo. Elapsed time can be displayed as bars and beats based on the sequence tempo. Digital Performer can generate a click based on the sequence tempo. It is possible to create a tempo map within the sequence that allows for tempo changes. The tempo map is also used for any quantization of audio or MIDI within the sequence.

A musical composition can be created in Digital Performer based on a metronomic click track. It is also possible to create a tempo map around a performance that was not originally recorded while being referenced to the Digital Performer click.

Setting the Sequence Tempo

There are four modes to control the tempo of a sequence. The simplest method to use is via the Tempo slider. The Tempo slider is located under the right-hand counter in the Control Panel window.

Drag the Tempo slider to change the sequence tempo. The Tempo slider sets a fixed tempo for the sequence. The factory default mode of a Digital Performer sequence is to be under the control of the Tempo slider.

The Tempo slider can also be set by tapping a key on the computer or via remote MIDI trigger. Tapping to set a tempo is an easy and quick way to find and set the desired tempo for the composition. The default key command for setting a tempo via tapping is the backslash key. Set a MIDI remote command for Tap To Enter Tempo in the Commands window.

To the right of the Tempo slider is a setting for the Current Beat Value. Click on this to change the click resolution. The default Current Beat Value resolution is a quarter note.

To the right of the Current Beat Value is the Current Tempo display. This shows the current beats per minute of the sequence. Click on the Current Tempo to highlight the field, and type in a new bpm value. It is also possible to click-and-drag up and down to change the bpm value. When tempo changes

Figure 4.18

are programmed into the sequence, the Current Tempo indicator will update to show the current sequence tempo.

The factory default tempo of a Digital Performer sequence is 120 bpm. The default meter is 4/4. The default Current Beat Value is set to a quarter note. These parameters can all be changed. Tempo, meter, and beat value can be changed at any time during the sequence. Tempo, meter, and beat value changes are programmed and stored in the Conductor track.

Tempo Control Modes

Tempo mode is set via the menu to the right of the BPM Indicator in the Control Panel. The choices are: Tempo Slider, Conductor Track, Tap Pad, and Remote Control. There is also a choice to Set Remote source.

Figure 4.19

The default Tempo Control mode of Digital Performer is the Tempo slider. The Tempo slider is set to represent a single tempo for the duration of the sequence. If there are no tempo changes in the sequence, Digital Performer does not need to be under the control of the Conductor track. If there are any tempo change events in the Conductor track, they will be ignored as long as Digital Performer is under the control of the Tempo slider.

If there are to be any programmed tempo changes in the Digital Performer sequence, the sequence must be under the control of the Conductor track in order to follow those tempo changes.

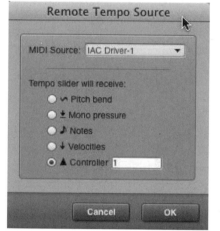

Figure 4.20

If Tap Pad is selected, a Tap Pad button is displayed to the left of the BPM Indicator. Tap on this button with the mouse to update the tempo. It is also possible to use a keyboard shortcut or remote MIDI message for tapping. When Tap Pad is engaged, Digital Performer will initially start playback at the current bpm value. Tap to slow down or speed up the sequence. This allows the sequence to be "conducted" in real time.

It is also possible to control sequence tempo via remote MIDI data. Program the type of data that is used to remotely control the Tempo slider via the Remote Tempo Source window.

The Conductor Track

Meter changes, click changes, and tempo changes are all stored in the Conductor track as events. By adding, deleting, or changing these events, you can program meter, tempo, and click changes into the sequence.

The contents of the Conductor track can be viewed in one of the graphic editor windows or in an Event List window. There are situations when one window or another may be the most efficient for working with data. For example, if the composer is working with tempo changes, it may be helpful to view the Conductor track in the

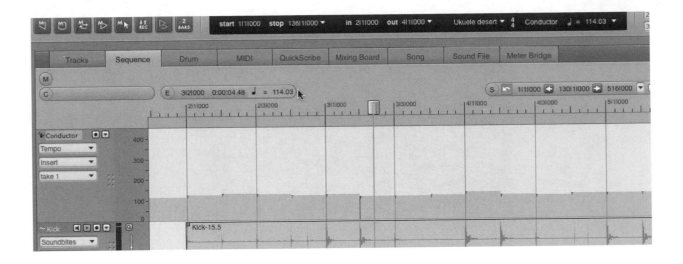

Figure 4.21

In other situations, it may be more obvious to view the contents of the Conductor track as a list of events. Open the Event List window from the Project menu or a sidebar window and display the Conductor track. All tempo, meter, or click changes are easy to spot and edit.

Creating and Editing a Tempo Map

If Digital Performer is under the control of the Conductor track but there is no tempo data entered into the Conductor track, the sequence will default to 120 bpm. If a tempo event is added after the start of the sequence, the tempo will be 120 bpm up until the point of the tempo change. To make a gradual tempo change, multiple tempo events are used to change the tempo over time.

Tempo changes can be created in the Sequence Editor window or the Event List for the Conductor track. In the Sequence Editor window, use the Pencil tool to draw in tempo changes.

- Display the Conductor track in the Sequence Editor window.

From the pop-up menu on the left, choose Tempo as the current data type.

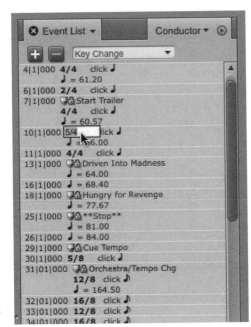

Figure 4.22

Figure 4.23

- Hold down the P key, or select the Pencil tool from the Tools window. Click once to enter a single tempo event. Click-and-drag to draw tempo changes.

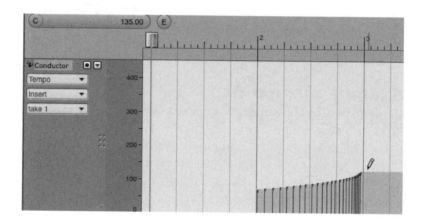

Figure 4.24

- To edit tempo events, change the mouse cursor back to the Arrow tool. Select individual or multiple tempo events and drag them up or down, or delete them.

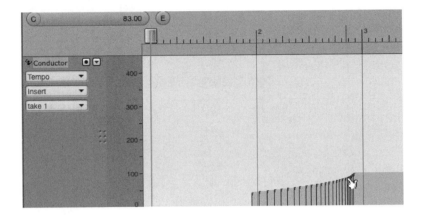

Figure 4.25

- Individual tempo events can also be selected and then edited with the Event Information display.

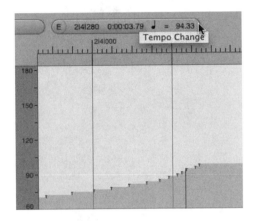

Figure 4.26

To enter tempo events in the Event List, choose the type of event to be entered, and press the + (plus) button. A tempo event will be added at the current counter location. Edit the event by clicking on it in the Event List window.

Figure 4.27

It is also possible to program meter and tempo changes with a variety of other tools throughout Digital Performer. For example, under the Project menu, select Conductor Track to see a range of programming options.

For example, to program a gradual tempo change from 100 to 120 bpm that happens between two specific locations in the sequence, Digital Performer can create the tempo change events. Go to the Project menu and choose Conductor Track > Change Tempo. This window provides a set of tools for creating tempo changes within the sequence.

Once a tempo map has been created, changes can be made to any part of the tempo map. Select Tempo Events in the Sequence Editor or Event List. Go to

Figure 4.28

the Region menu and choose Scale Tempo. This window provides a set of tools for changing the selected tempo events.

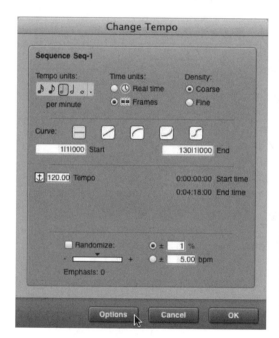

Figure 4.29

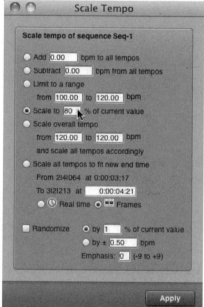

Figure 4.30

Meter

Meter describes the number of beats within a bar. For example, common time, also called 4/4 time, consists of four quarter-note beats per bar.

In Digital Performer, meter is used for beat and bar timeline display, and click functions. The default meter of a Digital Performer sequence is 4/4 time.

Meter changes are stored as events within the Conductor track.

Audio Tempo

So far we have been discussing the tempo of the sequence timeline. If audio or MIDI is recorded while listening to the Digital Performer click, the recorded performance will reference the tempo map of the sequence timeline.

MIDI notes do not contain any tempo data. MIDI data plays back at the tempo of the sequence timeline.

Audio files are different from MIDI in this regard. An audio file may or may not contain tempo information. Tempo data inside an audio file is important in order to accurately change the tempo of the audio. Tempo data is required in order to match the tempo of the audio to other audio or to the sequence tempo.

If audio is recorded in Digital Performer, tempo information will be embedded in the audio file that reflects the current sequence tempo. This means that if audio is recorded while referencing the Digital Performer click, the audio files will contain accurate tempo information. If audio is recorded without referencing the Digital Performer click, there will be tempo data embedded in the audio file, but it will not be an accurate reflection of the performance.

If an audio file is imported into Digital Performer, that audio file may or may not have embedded tempo data. Some commercially produced audio loops have embedded tempo data. Examples of audio loops with embedded tempo information include Acid WAV files and GarageBand's Apple Loops. Digital Performer can import these audio files and can use the embedded tempo data.

Changing the Tempo of Audio

If the sequence tempo is changed after MIDI is recorded, the MIDI data moves closer together or further apart to reflect the new tempo. However, audio works differently than MIDI when it comes to tempo. For example, if four bars of audio are recorded that contain a drumbeat, in order to change the tempo of those drums, the audio file needs to be shortened or lengthened. Tempo changing of audio within an audio file is done with time compression or time expansion of the audio file.

To do time compression or expansion of an audio file, Digital Performer creates a new audio file based on the original. This is called a *constructive edit*. When the new audio file is created, the original audio file is still on the hard drive. That allows the tempo change to be undone and reverted to the original audio file if needed.

Digital Performer can be programmed to automatically change the tempo of audio if it does not match the current sequence tempo. This preference is set in Preferences > Editing > Automatic Conversions. Enable Automatic Conversions for this project, and select the option to Convert To Sequence Tempo whenever file tempo does not match the sequence tempo.

If this option is set, any audio loops that are imported into Digital Performer that contain tempo data will be automatically converted to the current sequence tempo. Also, if this option is selected and the sequence tempo is changed, any audio currently in the sequence will be converted to the new tempo.

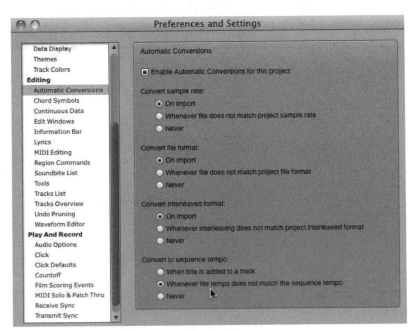

Figure 4.31

If the option is not set, it is possible to select audio that has embedded tempo data and choose Adjust Soundbites To Sequence Tempo from the Audio menu. This will convert the audio to the current sequence tempo.

There is also the option called Adjust Sequence To Soundbite Tempo. Select a soundbite that has embedded tempo data, and choose this command from the Audio menu. The sequence tempo data in the Conductor track will be changed to match the soundbite tempo.

POLAR

POLAR is an acronym that stands for Performance Oriented Loop Audio Recording. POLAR is a unique feature inside Digital Performer. Open POLAR by selecting it from the Studio menu. The default key command to open POLAR is Shift + P.

Figure 4.32

- POLAR is designed to record mono or stereo audio while the sequence cycles within a predetermined loop.
- POLAR allows multiple record takes to be created without having to touch any computer controls.
- POLAR records into RAM of the computer. At any time, the audio created by POLAR can be printed as audio files to the hard drive, as well as deposited into tracks within the Digital Performer sequence.
- POLAR can be used in the studio to easily create multiple takes or to build up complex overdubs.
- POLAR can also be used as a live-performance tool for creating and manipulating loops and layers on the fly.

Setting Up a Loop

POLAR relies on the Memory Cycle function to define its loop. Engage the Memory Cycle button and set the loop start and stop times.

Figure 4.33

The loop can be any length. The loop could be one bar long. The loop could be the entire length of the sequence. For example, let's say there is a 16-bar saxophone solo to be recorded. It could be desirable to set the loop start and stop points one bar before and one bar after the sax solo. That would give the sax player a bar before the solo and then a bar after the solo, each time the loop was repeated.

Configuring Input and Output

POLAR works in a manner similar to an audio track. Select the mono or stereo input to POLAR. Set the output of POLAR to the main monitor outputs. The input of POLAR can be changed on the fly, which allows different instruments to be recorded into a single POLAR session.

Recording in POLAR

POLAR has a Record button and a Play button. Typically, these controls are linked to the transport of Digital Performer. The Record button can be engaged or disengaged at any time.

There are two Record modes in POLAR. POLAR can begin recording as soon as the Record button is pressed. The alternative is that the Record button is pressed, but POLAR does not go into Record mode until the input signal exceeds a preset volume threshold. Choose between the two Record modes with the buttons on the left. Set the record gate parameters below.

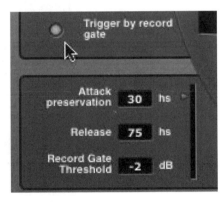

If POLAR is in gate trigger Record mode, it will go out of Record mode when the input signal drops below the gate threshold for a preset amount of time. The next time the input signal goes above the gate threshold, POLAR will go back into Record mode.

Figure 4.34

Creating Multiple Takes

POLAR allows "sound on sound" layering of audio into a single take. However, POLAR also allows multiple takes to be created on the fly. There are two ways to create a new record take in POLAR. A new take can be created manually. A new take can be created automatically if POLAR is in trigger mode, and the input signal goes above the gate threshold.

When a new take is created in POLAR, an additional option is to automatically mute the previous take. This means that if the goal is to create layers of harmonies, for example, all takes continue to be play-enabled as new takes are created. If the goal is to create multiple takes of a solo performance, each previous take can be muted when the next take is created.

Mixing in POLAR

Each take in POLAR can be muted or play-enabled. Each take in POLAR has a volume and pan control. This allows a stereo mix of selected tracks to be created on the fly.

Figure 4.35

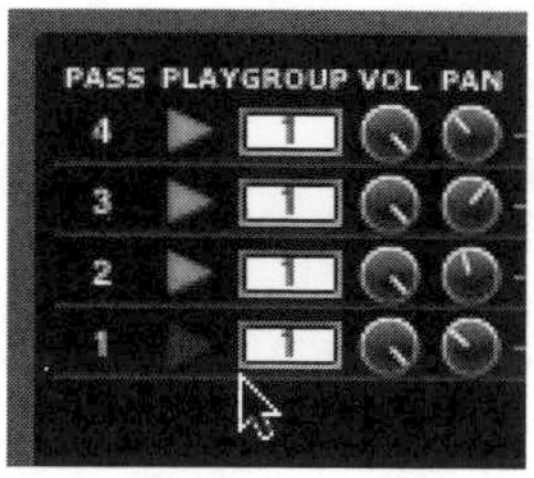

Printing from POLAR

The POLAR session, including all takes, can be saved as a separate file. Press the Save button to save the POLAR session.

POLAR takes can be exported as audio files. The Options button provides the export options.

If the Import option is set to "Add to tracks named POLAR," the selected takes will be added to the sequence. Each take will get its own new audio track. The takes will be exported to the exact location of the POLAR record loop.

Figure 4.36

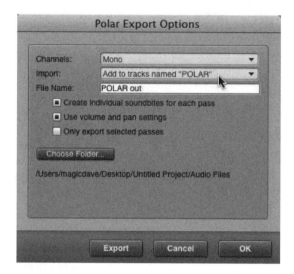

Figure 4.37

Chapter 5
EDITING

The basic techniques of computer-based music composition and production include recording, playback, mixing, and editing. This chapter will describe how to edit audio and MIDI in Digital Performer.

Although MIDI and audio are different types of data, Digital Performer is an integrated audio and MIDI sequencer. That means many editing operations work the same way with both audio and MIDI data.

There are many different ways to edit audio and MIDI in Digital Performer. Depending on what edit job needs to be done, there may be several choices on how to do that job. This chapter describes how to view, select, and edit audio and MIDI data in Digital Performer.

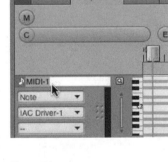

Figure 5.1

The Sequence Window

The Sequence window is the primary editing window for audio and MIDI in Digital Performer. The Sequence window looks similar to editing windows in other DAW software programs.

On the left side of the Sequence window, there is a pane that shows information for each track. Many of the same operations that can be done in the Tracks window can also be done in the Sequence window. For example, you press Option-click to rename a track.

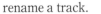

Figure 5.2

Click on the track type icon to change track color.

There are a series of pop-up menus that allow for input and output assignment and what type of data is visible frontmost in the track. For MIDI tracks it is possible to select the patch assignment. Data can be inserted by selecting the data type from the Insert pop-up menu, and then clicking or dragging in the track. It is also possible to create new takes for tracks, and to switch between those takes.

The Track Selector

The Sequence window can display any combination of tracks within the sequence. Tracks can be hidden or shown using the Track Selector. The Track Selector can be shown or hidden via the button on the bottom left-hand corner of the Sequence window. The default key command to open the Track Selector window is Shift + Command + T. Tracks that are highlighted in the Track Selector window will be visible in the Sequence window.

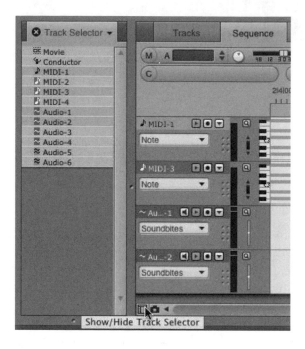

Figure 5.3

It is possible to set a preference so that a Track Selector list is visible within any window that can use the Track Selector. Set the preference in Preferences > Editing > Edit Window > Track Selector Button.

Zooming and Resizing

In the Sequence Editor window, tracks are displayed above and below each other. The order of the tracks can be changed by dragging a track up or down in the window.

It is important to understand how to zoom in or out to see more or less data in the window. Track size can be changed vertically and horizontally for all visible tracks. This is done with the plus and minus buttons in the bottom right-hand corner of the Sequence Editor window.

Figure 5.4

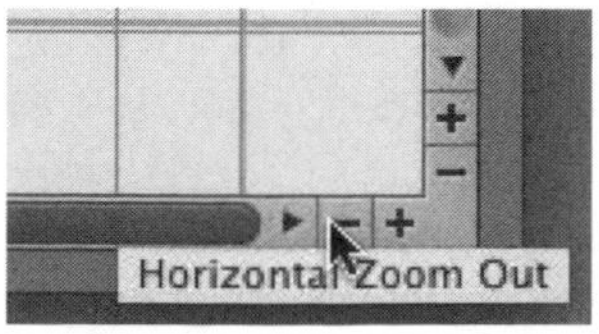

Figure 5.5

There are extensive zooming controls available via key commands.

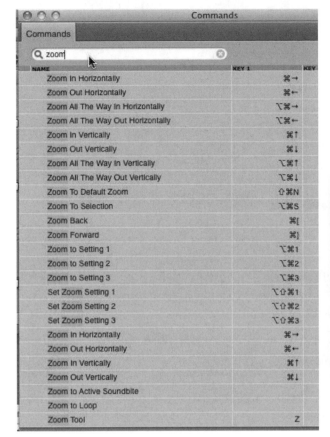

Figure 5.6

Figure 5.7

Tracks can be individually resized vertically by dragging on their left edge with the Hand tool. Option-drag on them to make all visible tracks the same size.

When the mouse cursor hovers over a soundbite or the time ruler, holding down the Option key will turn the cursor into a Magnifying Glass tool. Option-drag to zoom to the selected area.

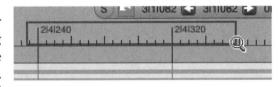

Figure 5.8

The Context-Sensitive Mouse Cursor

The mouse cursor changes its function inside the Sequence window depending on the position of the cursor. For example, move the mouse cursor over the gray pane on the left side of a track. When the cursor is on the bottom edge of the pane, it turns into a Hand tool. Click-and-drag with the Hand tool to change the vertical size of the track.

If the mouse cursor is positioned over the top two thirds of a soundbite, clicking-and-dragging will move the soundbite. Option-dragging will make a copy of the soundbite.

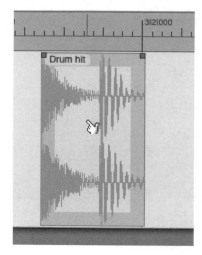

Figure 5.9

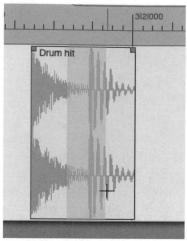

Figure 5.10

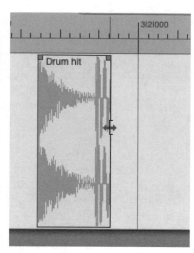

Figure 5.11

If the mouse cursor is positioned over the bottom third of the soundbite, it will become a Crosshair tool that can be used to drag and make a selection.

If the mouse cursor is positioned over the edge of a soundbite, it becomes an Edge Edit tool. The Edge Edit tool will hide or reveal the underlying audio of the sound file.

For a similar type of edit to MIDI notes, the mouse cursor turns into a Hand tool when placed on the left or right edge of a MIDI note. This allows the start or end time of a MIDI note to be adjusted.

If the mouse cursor is positioned on the top edge of a soundbite, it becomes a Crossfade tool. Click-and-drag to create a fade or crossfade.

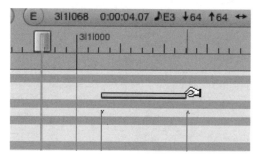

Figure 5.12

If the mouse cursor is positioned just below the Crossfade tool, it becomes a Hand tool that can be used to drag the edge of the audio to time-stretch or time-compress the audio.

The mouse cursor will also change its icon and function if a tool is selected from the Tools window. Tools can also be invoked with key commands.

Selecting Data

When working with a computer, there are two common functions that go together. The first step is to select data. The second step is to do something to the selected data.

Therefore, before any editing is done, data must first be selected. In Digital Performer,

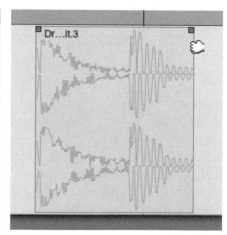

Figure 5.13   Figure 5.14

an individual MIDI message or single piece of audio is called an *event*. A selection can be a single MIDI or audio event, or it can be multiple MIDI or audio events. A selection can also be a time range that includes audio and MIDI events, as well as empty space.

There are many ways to make event and time range selections inside Digital Performer. Once data or a time range is selected, it can then be edited.

Time Range Selection

The first thing to understand about making a selection is the difference between a time range selection and a data selection. In Digital Performer, individual audio and MIDI events can be selected. It is also possible to make a time range selection, regardless of what data is in that time range. Clicking-and-dragging in the time ruler of a graphic edit window will make a time range selection. When a time range is selected, everything within that time range is selected, including any empty space.

For example, let's say the composer has left a bar of empty space at the beginning of the sequence. The music actually starts at bar 2.

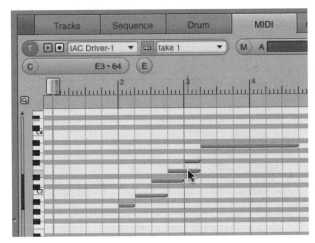

Figure 5.15

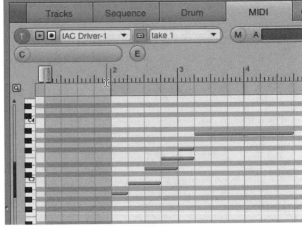

Figure 5.16

After working on the sequence, the composer decides to eliminate the bar of silence so that the sequence starts at bar 1. In the Tracks window, a selection is made by dragging within the time ruler.

From the Edit menu, the composer chooses Snip. The Snip command deletes the selected time range (and any audio or MIDI data in that time range), and moves everything to the right of the selection to what was the left edge of the selection.

For the next example, let's say the goal is to copy a bar of MIDI information from one place to another. In this example, MIDI data does not start at the beginning of the bar. However, when the data is copied and pasted, it needs to stay in the same relative position within the pasted bar. Therefore, it is possible to make a time range selection of exactly one bar, and paste that to another bar. The

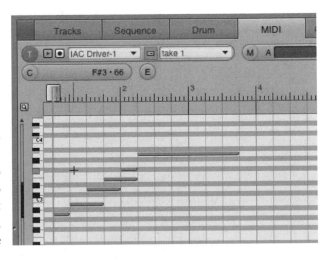

Figure 5.17

MIDI data will stay in the same relative position in the pasted location. In the picture below, the first step is to select one bar of time in the edit window. Do this by clicking-and-dragging in the time ruler of the edit window. All data within the time range is selected, along with the empty space at the beginning of the selection.

The second step is to copy the time range selection. Choose Copy from the Edit menu, or type Command + C on the computer keyboard to copy.

The third step is to define the new location where the time range selection will be pasted. This is done by making a new time range selection.

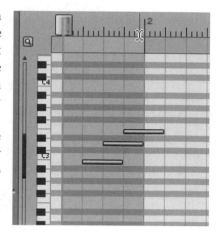

Figure 5.18

The last step is to paste the copied selection to the newly selected location. Notice how the MIDI data is in the same relative location in the new bar as it was in the original bar.

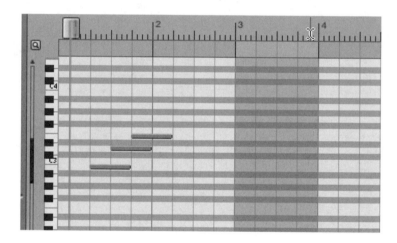

Figure 5.19

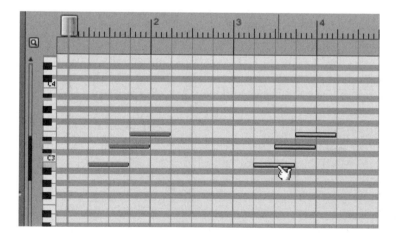

Figure 5.20

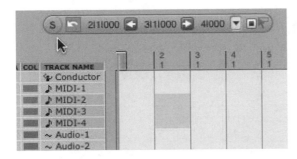

Figure 5.21

The Selection Information Window

All graphic editor windows in Digital Performer have a Selection bar in the top edge of the window. The Selection bar provides start and stop times for time range selections.

Click on the S in the Selection bar to open the Selection Information window. The Selection Information window can be opened in a sidebar window, or from the Studio menu. The default key command to open the Selection Information window is Control + I.

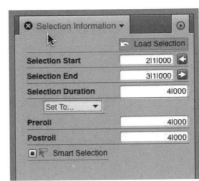

Figure 5.22

Object Selection

When a time range is selected, the entire time range, including all audio and MIDI events, will be highlighted. When individual audio and MIDI events are selected, only those "objects" will be highlighted. Any audio or MIDI event can be selected by clicking on it with the mouse. It is also possible to select multiple objects by clicking-and-dragging over the events with the mouse.

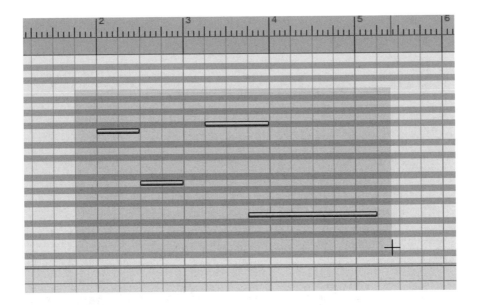

Figure 5.23

Shift-click to add or remove an object from the selection.

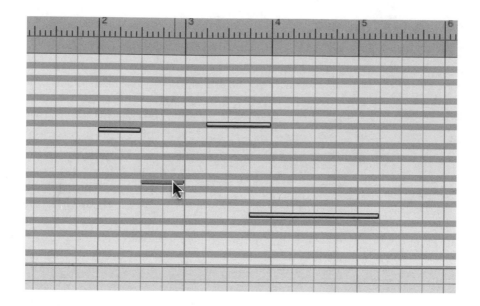

Figure 5.24

If the Control and Option keys are held down before clicking-and-dragging with the mouse, the mouse cursor turns into the Lasso tool. The Lasso tool allows the mouse to pass over part of an object, while selecting the entire object.

Here is an example of object selection: There is audio in multiple tracks and the goal is to delete several of these soundbites. If a time range selection is made, only the portion of the audio within the time range is highlighted.

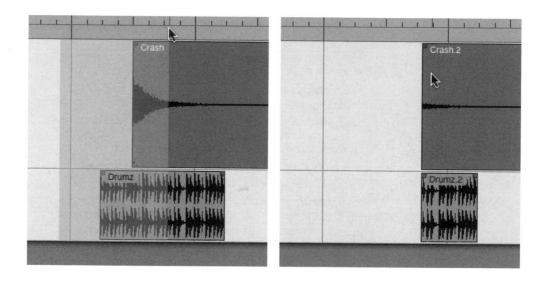

Figure 5.25   Figure 5.26

If the Delete key is now pressed, only the data in the highlighted time range will be deleted.

However, if the Lasso tool is used to make an object selection, all soundbites within the lassoed area are selected and highlighted. The Delete key will now remove all selected soundbites from the track.

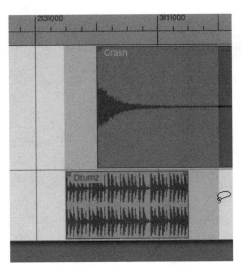

Figure 5.27

Edit Resolution

When making a selection in a graphic editor window, it is possible to "snap" the selection to a preset resolution. This can be useful if the goal is to make a precise time range selection. In the following example, Snap To Grid is enabled, allowing a precise selection of exactly one bar.

In the next example, Snap To Grid is disabled, and the time range selection is not constrained to any specific resolution.

Snap To Grid and Nudge

When editing within Digital Performer, it is possible to constrain edits to grid boundaries. It is also possible to set specific time increments for moving or nudging data within a track.

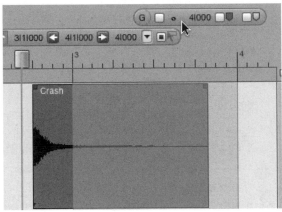

Figure 5.28

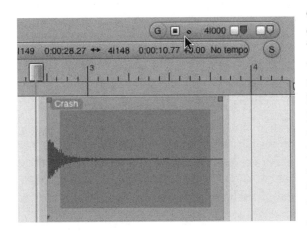

Figure 5.29

Snap To Grid can be enabled or disabled. This can be done by checking or unchecking the Snap To Grid button in an editing window. Snap To Grid can be temporarily enabled or disabled by holding down the Command key when selecting or dragging a time range. There is also a Snap Information window that provides options for time range selections. Open the Snap Information window from the Studio menu or within a sidebar window. The default key command to open the Snap Information window is Control + Shift + G.

The edit grid resolution can be changed at any time. Edit grid resolution can be based on the sequence grid, real-time increments, SMPTE frame time, markers, or beats found within an audio soundbite.

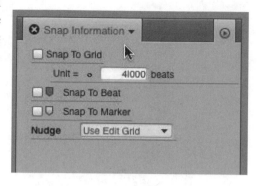

Figure 5.30

Nudging

In addition to making precise selections, the Snap To Grid function also works when moving data. If Snap To Grid is enabled, dragging data will move that data based on the grid resolution. When an audio or a MIDI event is moved by an amount specified in the Snap Information window, this is called Nudging. In addition to selecting and dragging data with the mouse cursor, selected data can also be nudged by using the Left or Right Arrow buttons.

Moving, Copying, Merging, and Pasting

Once audio or MIDI data is selected, it can then be deleted, moved, copied, pasted, or merged. Pasting data will remove all previous data from the paste location. Merge will add the copied data to the new location, while leaving any previous information that is still in the track. To paste or merge data to a specific location, that location must first be selected.

From the Edit Menu

Once data is selected, there is a range of options available under the Edit menu to move, copy, paste, delete, or merge data.

In a Graphic Editor Window

Audio and MIDI data can be moved or copied in a graphic editor window by dragging it with the mouse. Click-and-drag on any MIDI or audio event to move that event. In the Sequence editor, click on the upper portion of a soundbite to move it. Notice that the mouse cursor turns into a single finger icon when moving data.

Option-drag to make a copy of the audio and MIDI objects within the selection. Notice that when Option-dragging data, the mouse cursor changes to a two-fingered icon.

If Snap To Grid is enabled, the moved or copied data will follow the snap resolution as it is created. For example, if the edit resolution is set to whole notes, and a one-bar soundbite is option-dragged, that will create a duplicate of the soundbite that starts at exactly the next bar. This is a quick way to move or repeat a phrase of data in a track, while keeping the correct timing in relation to the sequence grid.

The Region Menu

A *region* is a time range or data selection. Functions under the Region menu will be applied to the selected time range and any data in that time range.

It is possible to select anything from a single MIDI note to the entire sequence, and then do a common operation to that data via the Region menu.

For example, let's say that the goal is to create a key modulation for the last 16 bars of the composition. The steps to do that job are as follows:

In the Tracks window, click-and-drag to select those last 16 bars of the sequence. Because the selection is made in the time ruler, all audio and MIDI tracks are included in the selection.

From the Region menu, choose Transpose. In the Transpose window, there are many options for how the transposition will work. For a simple modulation of one whole step, choose Interval, and a change from C3 to D3. This will cause all the selected audio and MIDI to be transposed up by a single whole step.

The MIDI Editor Window

The MIDI Editor window can be opened from a tab in the Consolidated window. It can be opened from the Project menu, via a shortcut, MIDI remote command, or key command. The default key command to open the MIDI Editor window is Shift + G.

Navigating the Window

The MIDI Editor window displays only MIDI tracks. The window is divided into an upper and lower portion. The upper portion of the window displays MIDI notes. The lower portion displays other MIDI data such as note velocities, MIDI controllers, pitch bend data, and patch changes.

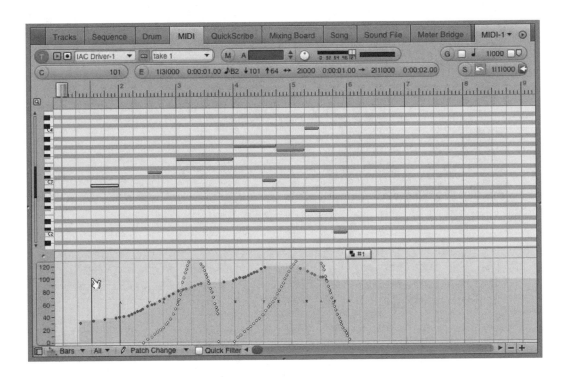

Figure 5.31

There's a significant difference between the way MIDI tracks are displayed in the MIDI Editor window as opposed to the Sequence Editor window. In the MIDI Editor window, multiple MIDI tracks are displayed superimposed on top of each other. This allows an "at a glance" view of how multiple MIDI tracks are working together in terms of rhythm and harmony. The MIDI Editor window also makes it easy to do similar edits to multiple MIDI tracks with a single operation.

Display and Edit Multiple Tracks

All current MIDI tracks are listed in the Track Selector for the MIDI Editor window. Highlighting multiple tracks causes those tracks to be displayed in the window. Visible layers are based on the order of the tracks in the Tracks window.

When multiple tracks are selected, it is possible to make a selection that includes data from the visible tracks. Click-and-drag in the time ruler or drag diagonally over data to select across multiple tracks.

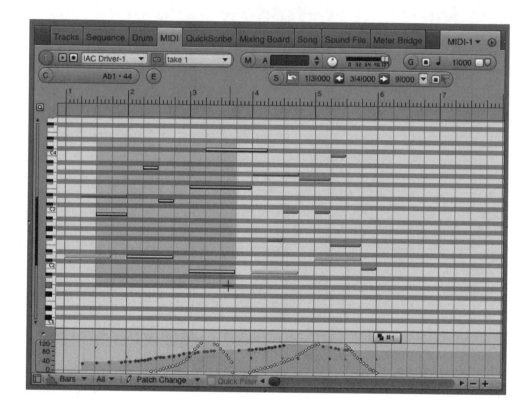

Figure 5.32

Any edit done to the selected data will be done to the data in all displayed tracks. For example, grab the right edge of a selected MIDI note and drag to make all selected MIDI notes longer or shorter.

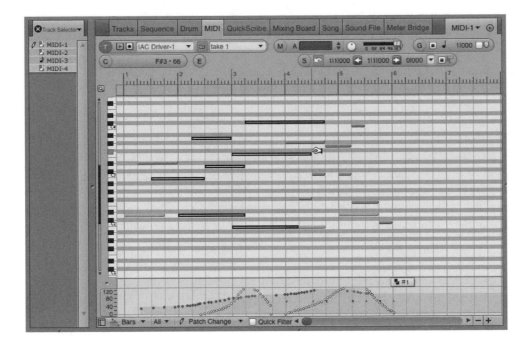

Figure 5.33

Assigning different track colors is an effective way to tell MIDI tracks apart in the MIDI Editor window.

The Master Edit Track

When multiple MIDI tracks are displayed, one track is the Master Edit Track. The Master Edit Track is denoted by the Pencil icon in the Track Selector.

Change the Master Edit Track by clicking to move the Pencil icon to a different track. The Master Edit Track determines which track will be edited by the Pencil tool.

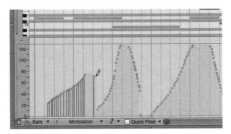

Figure 5.34   Figure 5.35

Inserting Data

The Pencil tool will draw MIDI data into the MIDI Editor window. The type of data that will be created is determined by clicking on the Insert Event Type menu on the bottom edge of the track.

Viewing Controller Data

There are two quick-view filters available in the MIDI Editor window. To the right of the Insert menu, there is a Quick Filter checkbox. If any data is currently selected, checking this box will hide all other data types. To the left of the Insert menu is a second view filter that will display only the selected data type. This makes it easy to view and edit all data of a specific type in a complex track.

There are three ways to view controller data in the MIDI Editor window. Click on the menu in the bottom left to change the view mode.

Controllers can be viewed as individual events in the Points mode.

Controllers can be viewed as individual events with a color bar connecting those events. The color bar extends left and right, making it easy to see the current value of a controller, even if it is offscreen.

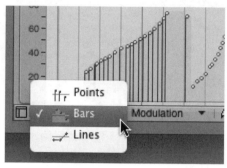

Figure 5.36

The third view mode is the Lines mode. This mode displays MIDI controller data in a manner similar to audio automation.

Dragging a point in Lines mode will create multiple MIDI events to make a smooth transition between those points.

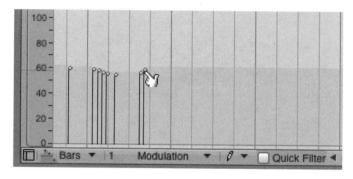

Figure 5.37

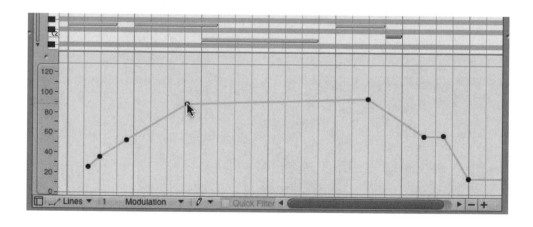

Figure 5.38

The Event List Window

Audio and MIDI data in Digital Performer is displayed either graphically or as a list of events. The contents of any track can be viewed in an Event List window.

Open an Event List Window

The factory default key command to open an Event List window is Shift + E. An Event List window can be opened in a sidebar window of the Consolidated window, or from the Project menu. To open an Event List window from the Project menu, first select one or more tracks in any edit window. An Event List window can also be opened by right-clicking on any track name in an edit window.

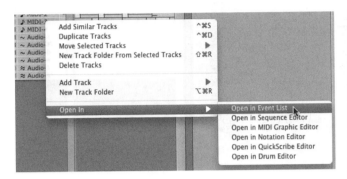

Figure 5.39

It is also possible to display multiple Event List windows simultaneously.

Switching Between Tracks

At the top right of an Event List window is a tab that allows the window to switch between which track is currently being viewed.

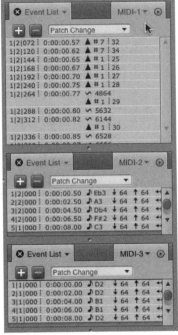

Figure 5.40

Viewing Data in the Event List

All data in a track is displayed sequentially in the Event List window. Each event displays its time within the sequence, what type of event it is, and other information about the event, such as MIDI note velocity or soundbite name.

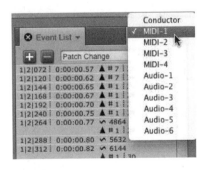

Figure 5.41

A significant difference between an Event List window and a graphic editor window is that in the Event List, all events are displayed one after another, regardless of where those events are in the sequence. For example, if there is a MIDI note at bar 1, and the next MIDI note is at bar 50, the two MIDI events will be right next to each other in the Event List.

The View Filter can be used to show or hide specific data types in an Event List window. For example, here is an Event List for a MIDI track that contains MIDI notes, pitch bend, and volume and modulation controller information. MIDI notes are represented by a Note icon. Pitch bend data is represented by a Wave icon. The controller data is represented by a Triangle icon.

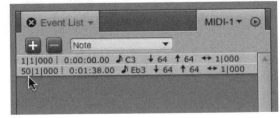

Figure 5.42

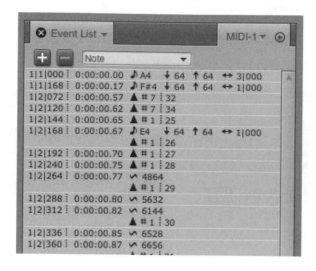

Figure 5.43

By using the View Filter, all events can be hidden except the pitch bend data.

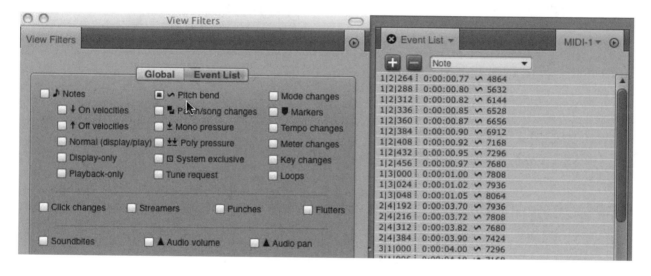

Figure 5.44

The pitch bend data can then be easily selected and deleted. When notes and controllers are reenabled in the View Filter, the Event List displays the remaining note and controller events.

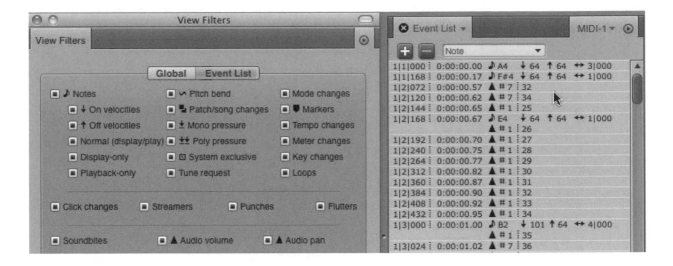

Figure 5.45

Selecting Events

Events can be selected by clicking with the mouse. Clicking-and-dragging up or down allows a range of events to be selected. Shift-clicking allows events to be added or removed from the selection.

Deleting and Adding Events

To delete an event or events, select the events and press the Delete key on the computer keyboard, or the – (minus) button (for Delete Event) at the top of the Event List. To add an event, choose the type of event from the pop-up menu and press the + (plus) button (for Insert Event). The new event will be added at the current counter location.

Editing Events

Double-click on any parameter in an event to "pop up" that parameter. Enter a new value and press Return to exit the Edit mode, or press Tab to go to the next editable field.

The Drum Editor Window

The Drum Editor window can be opened via a tab in the Consolidated window, or from the Project menu. The Drum Editor window can be opened via shortcut button, remote MIDI command, or key command. The default key command to open the Drum Editor window is Shift + D.

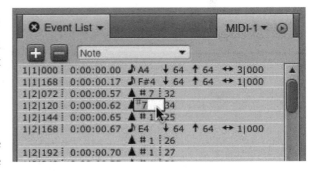

Figure 5.46

The Drum Editor window displays MIDI tracks with a grid-style editor. The resolution of the edit grid can be changed with the View Resolution button in the upper left-hand corner.

The purpose of the Drum Editor window is to provide an editing environment similar to the way a hardware drum machine works. Use the Pencil tool to click and add or delete MIDI notes in a grid to rhythmic patterns.

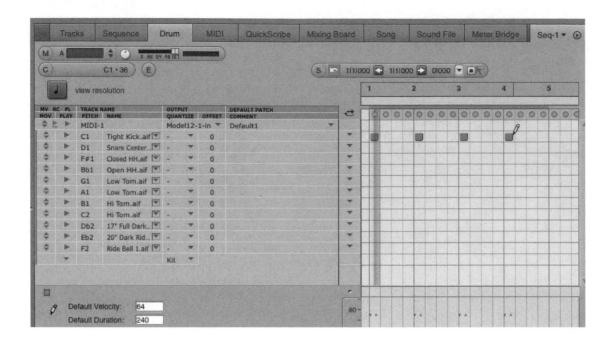

Figure 5.47

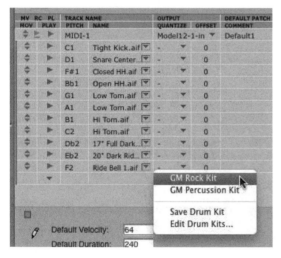

Figure 5.48

Displaying MIDI Tracks and Notes

Use the Track Selector to hide or show MIDI tracks in the Drum Editor window. Within a MIDI track, individual MIDI notes can be shown or hidden. This allows the Drum Editor window to display only MIDI notes that trigger actual drum sounds.

Click on the arrow below the MIDI track name to display a list of MIDI notes that are currently being used in the MIDI track. Selecting the notes will display them in the window. The same menu also allows a range of MIDI notes to be added to the display. Click on the field to the right of the arrow to add single notes to the display.

Use the Kit menu to automatically show a note map that corresponds to GM drum kit or percussion kit mapping. It is also possible to save and recall specific note displays via the Kit menu.

If there is a patch list available to the device that is assigned to MIDI track output, and if that patch list includes drum note names, the Drum Edit window can automatically display the drum note names. Select a patch for the MIDI device from the Default Patch column.

If the MIDI device assigned to the track output does not have a patch

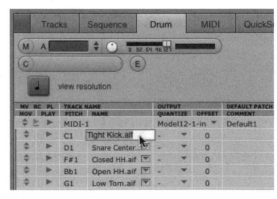

Figure 5.49

list or note names available, it is possible to type in the drum note names by Option-clicking in the Name field for each MIDI note.

Editing Notes

The Pencil tool can be used to add or delete notes. In Grid mode, added notes will be placed exactly on metronomic boundaries, and initially will have a default velocity value of 64 and duration of an eighth note.

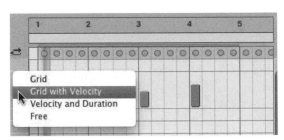

It is possible to edit velocity and duration of notes in the Drum Editor window. Click on the Display Mode menu to change the grid view to Grid with Velocity or Velocity and Duration.

It is also possible to nudge MIDI notes so they are not exactly on the sequence grid boundaries. Select "Free" in the Display Mode menu. Set the nudge amount in the Snap Information window. Select a note or notes and use the Left and Right Arrow keys to nudge the notes.

Figure 5.50

Muting and Quantizing Individual Drums Within a Kit

The Drum Editor window has the unique ability to mute all notes of a specific value in a MIDI track. This allows individual drums within the same MIDI patch to be muted or soloed.

Individual drums or groups of drums can be selected and nondestructively quantized within the track. For example, it may be desirable to quantize the kick drum but not the hi-hat. Select one or more drums and choose Quantize from the menu to the right of the drum note name.

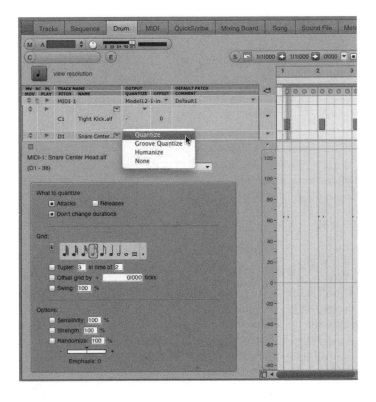

Figure 5.51

The Rhythm Brush Tool

In addition to using the Pencil tool to add notes in the Drum Editor window, it is also possible to use a Rhythm Brush tool to draw in patterns of notes. Patterns can be based on fixed values or grid settings. Patterns can be created from existing MIDI notes and stored for recall. Digital Performer also ships with a list of preset patterns.

For example, to paint in a hi-hat pattern, display the hi-hat drum note. Choose the Rhythm Brush tool from the Tool palette. Click on Custom in the Rhythm Brush Tool options. Choose a preset pattern from the pop-up menu. Click-and-drag with the Rhythm Brush tool to add the pattern to the hi-hat track.

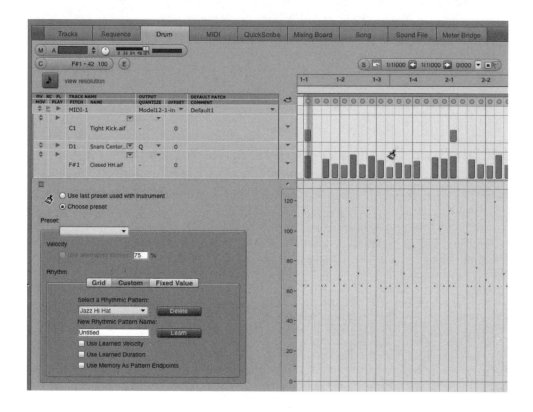

Figure 5.52

Editing Audio

Digital Performer provides complete tools for destructive and non-destructive audio editing. The following section describes the basic techniques for editing audio within Digital Performer.

Sound File Versus Soundbite

The first thing to understand when editing digital audio within Digital Performer is the difference between a sound file and a soundbite. A *sound file* is a specific file on the hard drive that represents digital audio. When Digital Performer records audio, it creates sound files. The sound files are separate from the Digital Performer session file. By default, sound files are stored in the Audio Files folder that is created inside the project folder.

A *soundbite* is a region within a sound file. A region is defined by start and stop time pointers inside the sound file. A sound file can contain many soundbites. In Digital Performer when audio is displayed in a track, it is a soundbite that is visible. This allows audio to be edited and moved around inside a track without having to alter the original sound file.

When audio is recorded into Digital Performer, a single soundbite is created that represents the entire length of the sound file. That soundbite and sound file are then represented in the Soundbites window.

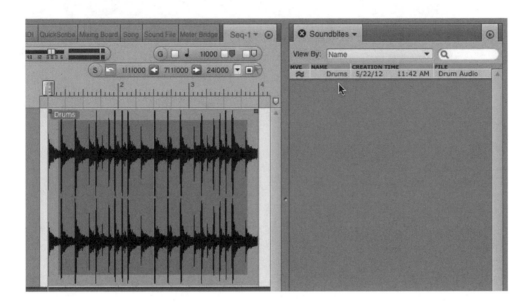

Figure 5.53

The soundbite can now be edited. For example, if the soundbite is cut with the Scissor tool, there will now be a total of three soundbites listed in the Soundbites window. This will include the original full-length soundbite, which is no longer in the track, and the two new soundbites that were created by the cut. Each soundbite has a different name, but all three soundbites belong to the same sound file.

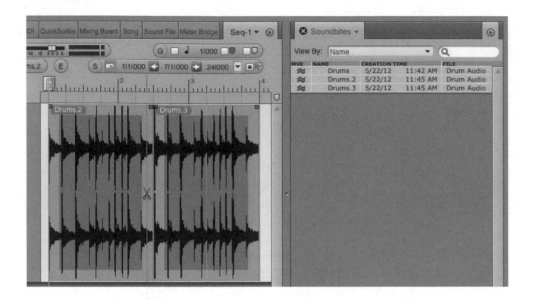

Figure 5.54

Nondestructive Editing

A nondestructive edit is an edit that changes audio in a track, but does not alter the sound file on the hard drive. Nondestructive editing allows audio to be changed at any time in a track without losing the data in the original sound file.

For example, the start and stop pointers within a soundbite can be changed to shorten or lengthen the soundbite within the sound file. One way to do this is to drag the right or left edge of a soundbite to hide or reveal the underlying sound file. This is called *edge editing*. This operation does not change the audio inside the original sound file, and is therefore a nondestructive edit.

Soundbites can be deleted from a track or moved around inside a track. Soundbites can be copied and duplicated. Because none of these edits change the audio information inside the sound file, these are all nondestructive edits.

Digital Performer also features pitch automation within audio tracks. Pitch automation changes the pitch of monophonic audio on playback without altering the original audio file.

Constructive Editing

A destructive edit is when data is changed on the hard drive. Because Digital Performer keeps an undo history of every edit, no audio edit is ever really completely destructive. As long as the Undo History is intact, the original audio is still available on the hard drive. Therefore a destructive edit in Digital Performer can be called a "constructive" edit, because new audio is being created with the edit.

Typically, destructive/constructive editing is done to change an audio waveform within a sound file. Changing the length of an audio file is also constructive/destructive.

Track Comping

Track comping is the process of assembling a single master take based on the best parts of multiple other takes. Digital Performer has powerful tools for managing multiple audio takes and creating master comp takes.

Takes can be controlled from the Tracks window or the Sequence window. In the Tracks window, click on the Take field for an audio track. In the Sequence window, click on the Take pop-up menu on the left edge of the track. This will open a menu with take options for that track.

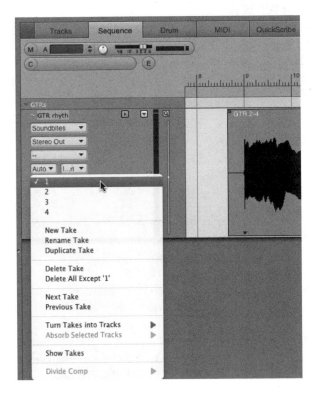

Figure 5.55

Multiple tracks can be consolidated into a single track as takes. Select the tracks and choose Absorb Selected Tracks > All Takes from the Take menu for one of those tracks.

Multiple takes within a track can be split out as their own audio tracks. For tracks that contain multiple takes, click on the Take menu and choose Turn Takes Into Tracks > All Takes.

In the Sequence window, there is an additional command in the Take > Options menu called Show Takes. Open the Sequence window and hide all tracks except a single audio track that contains multiple takes. Select Show Takes from the Take menu. The takes within the tracks will be displayed. The take that was currently enabled will be duplicated above the other takes. This is the *comp take*.

From the Tool palette choose the Comp tool. Click-and-drag to select a region in one of the original takes. The selected area will be copied to the comp take. Click in the same region for a different take, and that region will be copied to the comp take. This allows the selection of different regions from different takes to be added to the comp take.

Figure 5.56

Choose Hide Takes from the Take menu to hide the takes back inside the track, leaving the new comp take as the currently enabled take.

Fades and Crossfades

When editing audio, sometimes it is desirable to have fade-ins and fade-outs at the edit points. If audio is cut abruptly, there can be an audible pop at the edit point. If two soundbites overlap or abut each other, it may be desirable to have one soundbite fade in as the other fades out.

Digital Performer provides the ability to create nondestructive fades and crossfades for soundbites. The fade shapes are customizable. Fades and crossfades can be applied individually or to a batch of multiple edits.

Fades and crossfades can be created manually in the Sequence window. If the mouse cursor is positioned correctly at the top left or right edge of a soundbite, it will turn into the Fade icon.

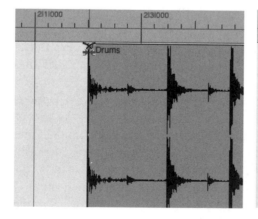
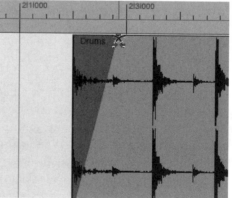

Figure 5.57   Figure 5.58

A fade or crossfade can then be created by dragging the fade point in the soundbite.
If multiple soundbites are selected, the Fade tool will create fades for all selected soundbites.

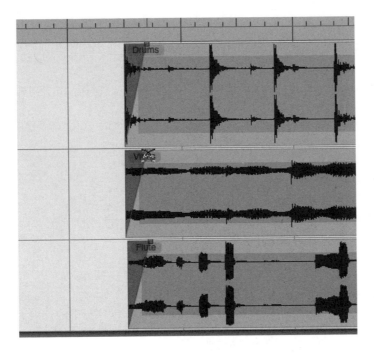

Figure 5.59

Fades and crossfades can also be made by making a selection and choosing Fade from the Audio menu. The Create Fades window will open. If multiple edit points are selected, you can apply fades to all of those edit points by pressing the OK button in the Fade window.

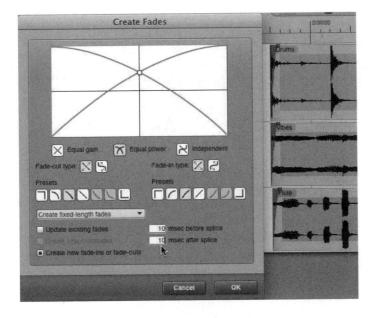

Figure 5.60

Soundbite Gain

Each soundbite can have volume automation embedded. The volume automation can be edited when the soundbite is viewed in the Sequence Editor window or Sound File Editor window when the Edit Layer view is set to Bite Volume.

The line through the waveform represents the volume of the soundbite. Initially, soundbite gain is set with no boost or cut.

One simple way to change soundbite gain is to select the soundbite and go to the Audio menu and choose one of the options from Bite Volume And Gain.

Figure 5.61

By clicking-and-dragging with the mouse, points can be created on the automation line that allow complex volume automation to be created.

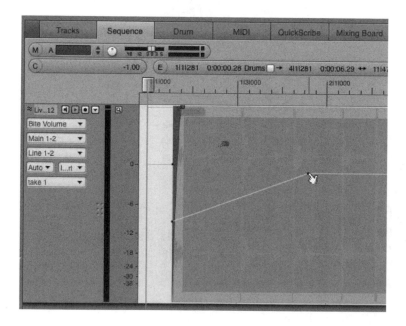

Figure 5.62

The volume automation is nondestructive. It is specific to the soundbite and can be changed at any time. If the soundbite is used in multiple places in the sequence, changing the bite volume will change it in all instances of that soundbite.

Soundbite gain changes can be printed to the soundbite by selecting the soundbite and choosing Merge Soundbites from the Audio menu. A new soundbite and sound file will be created, with the bite volume change printed.

Pitch Editing and Automation

Digital Performer provides several ways to change the pitch of digital audio. Pitch-shifting can be done to any audio, but the sonic results can vary depending on the quality of the audio. In general, radical pitch-shifts of polyphonic audio will not sound good. By comparison, more subtle changes to monophonic audio will generally be very high quality.

Audio can be selected and pitch-shifted via the Transpose window under the Region menu. The Transpose window is the same window that is used for MIDI transposition, and all the MIDI transposition functions are available for audio pitch-shifting.

It is also possible to nondestructively automate pitch directly inside a soundbite. Pitch automation is similar to having a plug-in running inside the soundbite. Changes made to the pitch are nondestructive playback effects and can be deleted or altered at any time. It is possible to print pitch automation to the soundbite.

The pitch automation function is designed to be used with monophonic audio. This is a powerful feature for correction of intonation. Pitch automation can be used to change individual notes within a performance. Pitch automation can be used to create harmonies. Pitch automation can even be used to completely rewrite melodies.

To display the pitch automation function in an audio track, select Pitch from the pop-up menu on the left.

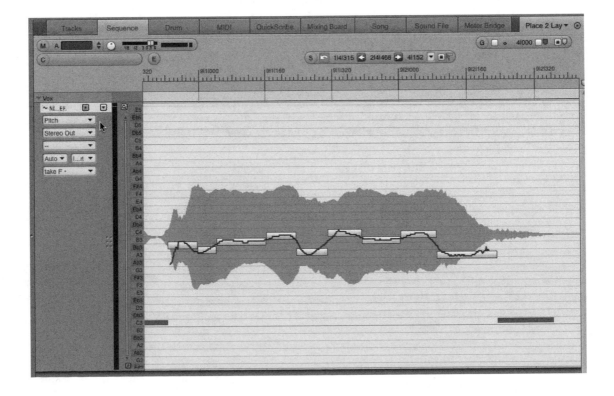

Figure 5.63

The track will now display the audio waveform in the background and two additional pieces of information in the foreground. The actual pitch of the monophonic audio is displayed as a blue line. Behind the blue line are blocks that are called *pitch segments*.

Pitch segments represent Digital Performer's interpretation of the audio pitch as individual notes. The pitch segment sensitivity is adjustable. For example, the vibrato of a note could be interpreted either as many different notes or as a single note, depending on the sensitivity of the pitch segment detection. Select a region of the audio, go the Audio menu, and choose Pitch Automation > Adjust Pitch Segmentation. A window with a slider will open that allows adjustment of the pitch segments.

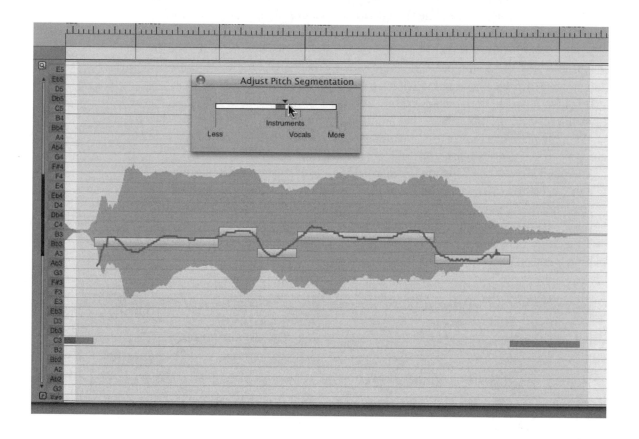

Figure 5.64

It is also possible to manually cut or connect pitch segments. To cut a pitch segment, use the Scissor tool or hold down the C key and click with the mouse.

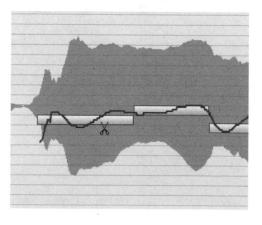

Figure 5.65

To connect pitch segments, use the Mute tool or hold down the M key and click with the mouse.

Pitch segments are used as guides for controlling pitch. Click-and-drag up or down on a pitch segment, and it will snap to a note division. Hold down the Command key to move the pitch segment without snapping.

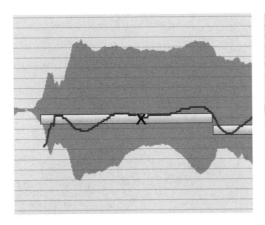

Figure 5.66

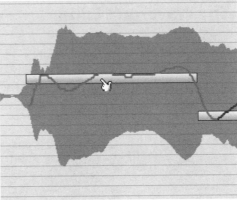

Figure 5.67

When any pitch automation is done, the blue pitch line turns red to indicate that an edit has been made. At any time, the pitch automation can be selected and deleted.

The pitch segment can also be used as a guide for pitch correction. Hold down the Option key to get the Pitch Scale tool. Drag up or down to conform the pitch to the pitch segment.

Pitch can be manually redrawn using the Pencil tool from the Tool palette. The Pencil tool can be controlled via a Reshape tool. In this example, pitch has been redrawn using a sine wave Reshape tool.

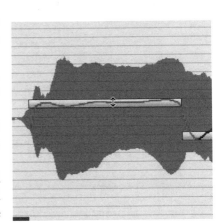

Figure 5.68

Pitch automation can be printed to the soundbite by selecting it and choosing Merge Soundbites from the Audio menu.

Merge Soundbites

If there are multiple soundbites in a track, it is possible to create a new piece of audio based on the selected soundbites or time range. Select a time range or specific soundbites in an audio track. Go to the Audio menu and choose Merge Soundbites.

A new sound file will be generated. The existing soundbites will be removed from the track, and a new soundbite will show up. The original soundbites and their sound files are still intact on the hard drive and referenced in the Soundbites window.

Figure 5.69

113

The newly created audio will include any soundbite gain edits, any pitch automation edits, and any fades or crossfades. These edits will all be printed to the newly merged audio. The merge will not include any plug-ins or track automation.

Merging soundbites is a useful technique if there are edits in a track, and that track needs to be exported as a single audio file. Merging soundbites can be done within multiple tracks with a single operation.

The Waveform Editor

Constructive/destructive audio edits are done primarily in the Waveform Edit window. An example of a constructive/destructive edit is redrawing the audio waveform with the Pencil tool. This type of edit is not done in the track. To redraw the waveform, the audio must be opened in the Waveform Edit window. Hold down the Command key and double-click on a soundbite to open that soundbite in the Waveform Edit window.

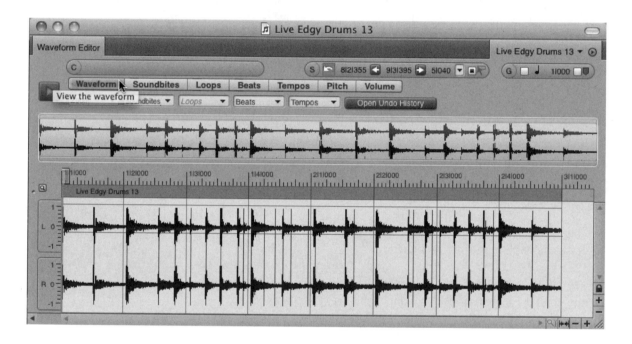

Figure 5.70

Use the + or – (plus or minus) buttons or Option-drag to zoom in on the waveform. Use the Pencil tool from the Tools window to redraw the waveform.

Select any portion of the waveform and choose Normalize from Audio > Waveform Editor. This will increase the gain of the selected audio so that the loudest transient is at maximum volume.

Select any portion of the waveform and choose Fade In or Fade Out from Audio > Waveform Editor to create fades.

Time-Stretching and Compression

Digital Performer can stretch or lengthen audio files. Digital Performer can change the tempo of audio without changing its pitch or tone. There are many ways to manipulate tempo of audio in Digital Performer. One direct method is by dragging the left or right edge of a soundbite to stretch or compress it.

When the mouse cursor is positioned correctly on the left or right edge of the soundbite, it will turn into a Hand tool.

When the mouse is then clicked-and-dragged left or right, that will stretch or compress the soundbite. There will be a ghost image of the soundbite until the mouse cursor is released.

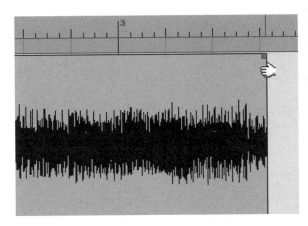

Figure 5.71

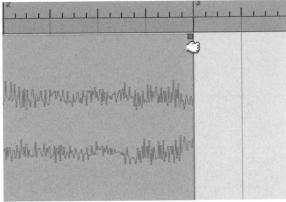

Figure 5.72

When the mouse is released, Digital Performer will create a new soundbite that is stretched or compressed to that point.

Quantizing

Quantizing means moving selected events in relation to a preset grid. Simple quantization moves all selected events to the nearest sequence grid, based on the grid resolution. It is possible to quantize MIDI events, automation events, soundbites, and even audio beats within soundbites. Quantizing is used to "fix" the timing of MIDI and audio performances.

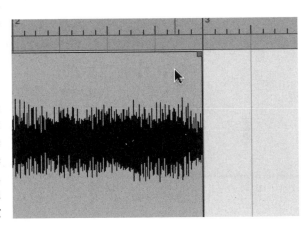

Figure 5.73

The Quantize Window

The Quantize window will affect data in a selected region. The Quantize window can be opened via remote MIDI message, via a shortcut, from the Region menu, or via a key command. The default key command for the Quantize window is Command + 0.

The Quantize window offers many options. The quantize grid can be set, including triplet and dotted-note resolutions. It is possible to set quantization strength or randomize the quantization to retain a "human" feel. It is also possible to set an offset to create a swing feel.

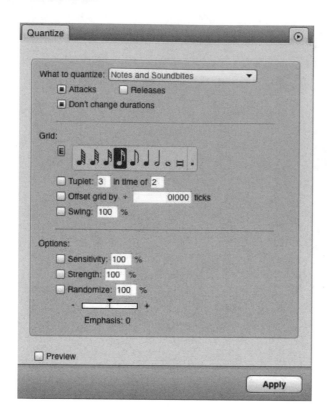

Figure 5.74

Quantizing MIDI

When MIDI is quantized, the MIDI events are moved within the track. It is also possible to quantize the start and end times of MIDI notes, which will change their durations.

To quantize MIDI notes, select the MIDI notes to be quantized. Next, select Notes from the pop-up menu in the Quantize window. Choose the desired quantize options and click Apply. The selected MIDI events will be moved to the quantized locations in their tracks.

The following figure shows a major scale played in quarter notes. Note that the notes do not all start exactly on the quarter-note grid of the sequence timeline.

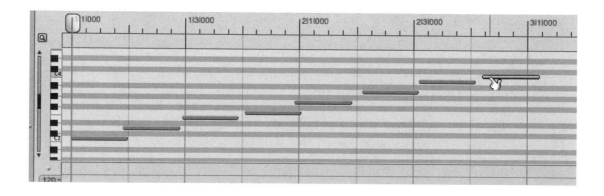

Figure 5.75

The next figure shows the same notes after being quantized to a quarter-note grid.

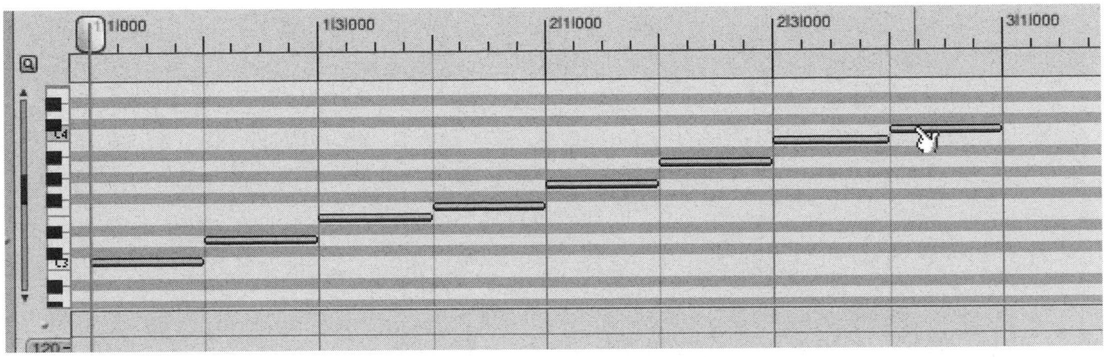

Figure 5.76

When quantizing, it may be possible to select the entire contents of a track and do the same quantize operation to all notes. However, it might also be possible that some notes need to be quantized to a specific grid resolution, and other notes need to be quantized to a different resolution. In some cases, no quantization may be required at all. Therefore, quantization can be applied to regions of data as needed. In the next example, there are MIDI notes quantized to an eighth-note grid. After that is a phrase of highlighted MIDI notes that are quantized to a triplet resolution. At the end of the example is a glissando of notes that are not quantized at all.

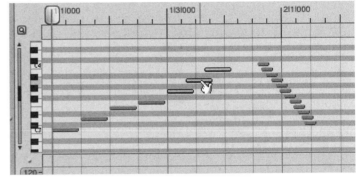

Figure 5.77

Quantizing Soundbites

Soundbites can be quantized just like MIDI events. To quantize soundbites, select a region that includes them, then in the Quantize window, choose Soundbites from the pop-up menu.

Quantizing Audio Beats

Digital Performer can quantize audio within a soundbite. This is done by identifying transients in the audio and moving those transients with time-compression or time-stretching of the audio within the sound file. Transients within audio are referred to as *beats*. By default, Digital Performer searches for beats in all newly recorded or imported audio.

The beat detection in Digital Performer is very sensitive. The sensitivity can be adjusted. For example, if a drummer hits a partially closed hi-hat cymbal, the hats will swish back and forth as they decay. This can be detected as multiple beats, even though it is a single hit. When quantizing audio inside a soundbite, it is very important to know which audio transients will be moved. Therefore it is possible and usually desirable to edit the beat map of a soundbite.

Press Command and double-click on a soundbite to open it in the Sound File Editor window. Click on the Beats tab to display the found beats in the soundbite. Beats are displayed as blue vertical lines over the audio waveform. If no beats are displayed, select the soundbite (Command + A) and choose Find Beats In Selection from the Beats menu.

Beats can be muted, which means they will not be used for any quantization operation in the audio. There are two ways to mute or unmute found beats within a soundbite. Select the soundbite and choose Adjust Beat Sensitivity or Adjust Beat Detection from the Audio menu. These two windows use different algorithms to do the same job. Move the slider in the window to adjust which beats are muted or unmuted.

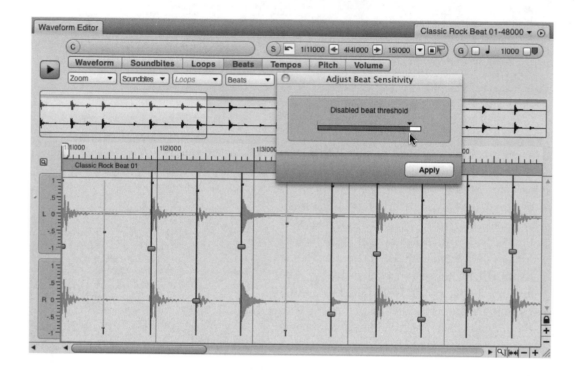

Figure 5.78

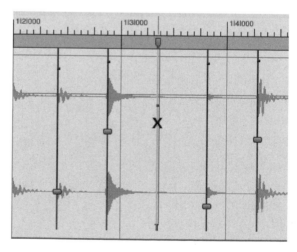

Figure 5.79

It is also possible to manually select beats to be muted or unmuted. Hold down the M key and click on a beat to mute or unmute it.

The beats that are left active are the ones that will be used to quantize the transients within the audio. Therefore, it is a good idea to look closely at the current beats in the soundbite before doing any quantization.

The View Filter

The View Filter is available from the Setup menu. The factory default key command to open the View Filter is Command + F. There are separate View Filter settings for Global windows and Event List windows.

In Digital Performer, it is possible to hide audio and MIDI data so that it is not visible. The data is still there and will play back, but if the data is hidden, it can't be selected. Hiding data can also be useful for simplifying what is visible in the track.

Hiding data is useful when making a selection if not all the data in the region is to be selected. For example, the following figure shows an audio track that contains soundbites and automation events. The soundbite is in the foreground, and the volume and pan automation is behind the soundbites.

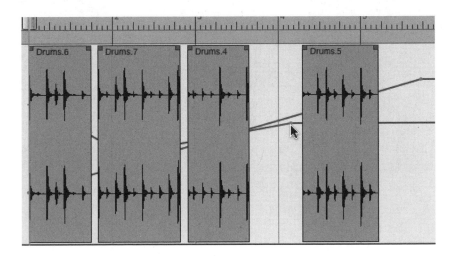

Figure 5.80

From the View Filter, uncheck Soundbites. If the soundbites are hidden, only the automation is left visible.

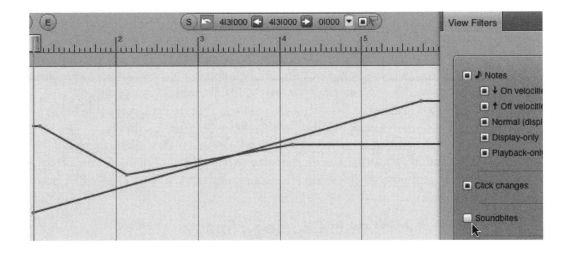

Figure 5.81

This makes it easy to select all of the visible automation data, but not the hidden soundbites. Press Command + A or choose Select All from the Edit menu to select all visible data. The automation data is selected. Press the Delete key to deleted the selected automation data. In the View Filter, enable soundbites, and the soundbites reappear, without any automation data left in the track.

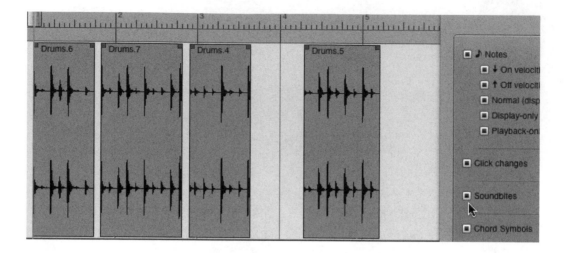

Figure 5.82

A common mistake that can be made is to hide data with the View Filter, and then forget that has been done. The result is that the sequence plays, but no data is visible within the sequence. If this ever happens, go to the View Filter window and make sure all data types are enabled.

The Clippings Window

Digital Performer provides the option to create Clippings windows. A Clippings window is initially an empty window. A Clippings window is used to hold aliases to audio/MIDI selections, effects presets, files, and applications. These aliases can be recalled as needed.

To create a Clippings window, go to Project > Clippings, and choose one of the three clipping window types. A new empty window will open that is initially called Untitled. Option-click on the name of the clipping window to rename it. Clipping windows can be closed, and then reopened by selecting them from Project > Clippings.

Drag any file or application into a clipping window to create a clipping alias of that file or application. Double-click on the clipping to launch the file or application. Drag a soundbite or multiple soundbites from the Soundbites window into a clippings window to create clipping aliases of those soundbites.

The Digital Performer Clipping Window

A Digital Performer clipping window will be available for all Digital Performer sessions. Digital Performer clipping windows are used to hold aliases that are useful for any session. For example, a Digital Performer clipping window could be used to store a library of sound effects samples that a composer might want to have available for any sequence.

The Project Clipping Window

A Project clipping window will be available only within the session in which it was created. Project clipping windows are used to hold aliases and data that are specific to that session. For example, if a clipping window is used as an Arrangement tool for a sequence, it would be typical to use a Project clipping window for that job.

The Startup Clipping Window

A Startup clipping window is used to store aliases of files or applications that will launch as soon as Digital Performer is launched. Think of this as a "startup items" folder for Digital Performer.

Arranging with Clippings

It is possible to select a region or tracks in a sequence and store that as a clipping. That clipping can then be dragged back into a sequence at any location. This allows clippings to be used as an Arrangement tool.

Create a new Project clipping window. This window will be used to hold onto regions of the sequence. Make a selection in any edit window. This can include any time duration and any combination of tracks in the sequence. Go to the Edit menu and choose Copy To Clipping Window. A submenu will appear with a list of currently available clipping windows. Select a clipping window and the selection will appear in that window as a single alias. The selection alias can then be renamed by Option-clicking.

The selection alias can then be dragged back into the sequence. The selection alias must be dragged back into the same track configuration as the one in which it was created. In other words, a selection clipping that contains audio cannot be dragged into a MIDI track. If the selection clipping includes data from multiple tracks, the clipping can only be dragged back into the same configuration of tracks.

Chapter 6
VIRTUAL INSTRUMENTS

Computers are capable of generating sound. This basic technology has been developed to the point that a computer can function as a musical instrument. A virtual instrument is a piece of software that generates sound.

Typically, virtual instruments work like traditional hardware MIDI sound modules. A virtual instrument can be triggered live by a controller such as a keyboard or drum pads. A virtual instrument can be triggered by a MIDI track. The MIDI data is routed to the virtual instrument. The virtual instrument generates sound. Digital Performer is a recording studio. Using virtual instruments is one way to generate sound inside that studio.

Virtual instruments have become a fundamental part of music composition and production. Virtual instruments allow a composer to create an audio production without the need for live musicians or hardware sound generators.

Virtual instruments are now also being used extensively in live performance. A musician can use a computer and a hardware MIDI controller to trigger and play any sound. Digital Performer can work as a host for virtual instruments in a live performance setting.

Digital Performer includes six different virtual instruments and has the ability to host additional virtual instrument plug-ins. This chapter will discuss virtual instruments and how they function with Digital Performer.

CPU and RAM

Running virtual instruments is one of the most demanding tasks a computer-based DAW is asked to do. Virtual instruments require CPU power to work, and in the case of sample-based instruments, they can use a great deal of RAM.

The power of the computer and the amount of available RAM will dictate how many simultaneous virtual instruments you can run. If the computer runs out of RAM of CPU power, the symptoms can include overall sluggish performance, audio artifacts, error messages, and even crashing.

All computers have a limit as to what they can do. The best solution for managing an efficient system is to understand how the system works. If there is a noticeable change in performance or stability, running fewer virtual instruments can solve that problem. If the output of a virtual instrument is printed as an audio track, the instrument can then be disabled. Playing an audio track requires far fewer computer resources than does triggering a virtual instrument.

Latency

When a virtual instrument is triggered, the computer takes time to generate audio, then pass that signal through any processing, and finally send it to an audio output. No matter how powerful the computer, it takes time to get from the moment the audio signal is generated by the instrument to when that signal finally arrives at an audio output and the monitor speakers. This time delay is called *latency*.

It is important to understand that latency delay happens only when an instrument is being triggered by a live MIDI signal. If the MIDI signal is being played back from a MIDI track, Digital Performer can calculate the time delay and compensate for that delay. This is called *automatic delay compensation*.

Delay compensation cannot be used to anticipate a live triggered MIDI signal. When a virtual instrument is triggered by a live MIDI keyboard, there will be a delay before the sound comes out of the monitor speakers. The good news is that this delay can be adjusted, and can be lowered to the point that the human ear cannot detect any delay.

For the average musician, any delay below 7 to 8 ms is undetectable by ear. If a guitar player is standing ten feet away from his or her amplifier, there will be a 10 ms delay between when the guitarist picks a note and when the sound of the amp gets back to the guitarist's ears. With Digital Performer the best trigger-to-audio performance for virtual instruments can be as low as 3 ms.

Latency delay is controlled by a specific setting within Digital Performer. Go to Setup > Configure Audio System > Configure Hardware Driver. This will open the Audio Hardware Driver window.

The buffer size setting is what determines the latency delay of virtual instrument plug-ins within Digital Performer. A lower buffer size means a lower trigger latency. A higher buffer setting means a greater latency delay.

The reason the buffer size is variable is because a lower buffer size puts a greater load on the computer CPU. Raising the buffer size eases the load on the CPU. When virtual instruments are being triggered live, the buffer size needs to be set low in order for the musician to be able to play the virtual instrument with no noticeable delay. However, it may be desirable to raise the buffer size so that the computer has more power for final mixdown. Remember, latency delay happens only during live triggering of instruments. Once the MIDI tracks have been recorded, Digital Performer plays back those tracks and virtual instruments with no latency delay.

For live triggering of virtual instruments, set the buffer size to no higher than 128. If the computer is powerful enough, drop the buffer size to 64 for the tightest possible timing.

Definition of a Virtual Instrument

The virtual instrument generates audio. The audio output of the virtual instrument can be routed, recorded, processed, and mixed like any other audio signal.

Types of Instruments

Virtual instruments use different methods to produce audio. Two of the most common methods used are synthesis and sample playback.

Synthesizers

A synthesizer makes sound from basic audio building blocks. There many different ways that sound can be synthesized.

A common technique used to generate sound is called *subtractive synthesis*. Subtractive synthesis starts with some sort of generated waveform. The waveform is shaped with amplitude envelopes, filters, LFOs, and other functions. Examples of subtractive synthesizers include the classic MiniMoog and most other analog synthesizers manufactured before 1980.

Another technique to synthesize sound is called *frequency modulation* (FM) *synthesis*. With FM synthesis, a waveform is generated, and the other generated waveforms are used to modulate the "carrier" waveform. FM synthesized sounds are obviously different than subtractive synthesized sounds. FM synthesized sounds have distinctive bell-like timbre. FM became a popular synthesis method in the 1980s. A classic example of an FM synthesizer is the Yamaha DX7.

Sample-Based Instruments

A sample-based instrument plays back recordings or *samples*. For example a sample-based instrument could play back recordings of actual piano or violin notes. Because the sound generated by a sample-based instrument is a recording, the quality of the sound produced by the instrument is dependent on the quality of the original sample recordings.

Sample-based virtual instruments are most often used to re-create the sounds of real acoustic instruments. In order to produce the most realistic playback, the maker of a sample-based instrument may make many different sample recordings of the original instrument. For example, a sample-based instrument that makes a piano sound may have recordings of each note on the piano keyboard. There may be multiple recordings of each note at different volumes. There may be additional sets of samples for when the sustain or damper pedals on the piano are pressed.

Sample-based instruments can take up a great deal of hard drive space to store all the individual samples. When a sample-based instrument is loaded and ready for playback, at least part of the instrument samples are loaded into the computer RAM. This is the reason that a large amount of RAM may be required for running sample-based instruments. These instruments may also take advantage of a technique called *disk streaming*. Disk streaming is when a portion of the instrument samples are loaded into RAM. When a sample is triggered, the instrument will stream the rest of the sample from the hard drive.

Hybrid Instruments

A hybrid instrument uses a combination of sampling and synthesis to produce sound. Sounds made by hybrid instruments have an acoustic quality because of the sampling, but also have synthetic qualities added in.

Instruments with Built-In Sequencers

Some instruments can generate sound without requiring a MIDI message to trigger the sound. An example of this is a drum machine.

A drum machine generates drum sounds. A drum machine may also have the ability to play back patterns. When the sequence plays, the pattern inside the drum machine plays in sync with the rest of the sequence.

Plug-Ins

A plug-in is a small piece of software that runs inside of a larger piece of software. In the case of a virtual instrument, if that instrument runs inside Digital Performer, it is running as a plug-in.

Digital Performer ships with six built-in virtual instrument plug-ins. Digital Performer can also host third-party virtual instrument plug-ins.

There are different software standards for virtual instrument plug-ins. On the Mac, Digital Performer supports MAS, VST, and Audio Unit format plug-ins. On Windows, Digital Performer supports MAS and VST format plug-ins.

ReWire Instruments

Digital Performer can work with other applications via the ReWire protocol. ReWire provides audio and MIDI communication between Digital Performer and other ReWire software.

A common example of a ReWire program is Reason software, made by Propellerhead Reason can be used to provide virtual instruments to Digital Performer.

For Digital Performer to work with Reason, or other ReWire software, first launch Digital Performer, and then launch Reason. This will make Digital Performer the ReWire master. Create an aux track in Digital Performer and set its inputs to a pair of audio returns from Reason. It will now be possible to assign the outputs of MIDI tracks in Digital Performer to the inputs of MIDI devices in Reason.

Instruments Included with Digital Performer

Digital Performer ships with a complement of built-in virtual instruments. Following is a description of each of the included instruments.

Bassline

Bassline is a monophonic synthesizer. It is modeled on the MiniMoog synth from the 1970s. Bassline uses a single oscillator and single filter. The output of Bassline is monophonic, but there is a detune feature that will provide a stereo output effect. Be sure to check out the factory preset patches.

Model 12

Model 12 plays back drum samples. It is possible to load 12 different drum samples into a single instance of Model 12. Entire kits can be loaded via a preset patch.

Figure 6.1

Individual drums samples can be loaded into each drum slot.

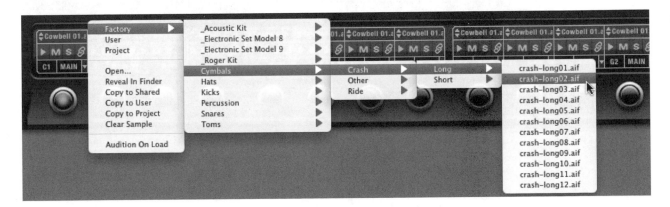

Figure 6.2

Each drum sound is triggered by a different MIDI note. The MIDI note can be changed by clicking-and-dragging up or down.

Figure 6.3

Individual drums can be muted or soloed. Each drum sound can be sent to a separate output via a bus.

Drums sounds can be locked together so that one sound will mute the other. This is useful for a hi-hat sound in which the closed hi-hat will mute the open hi-hat.

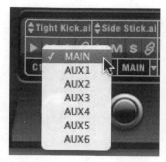

Figure 6.4

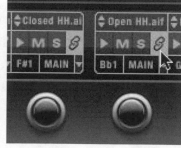

Figure 6.5

Drums can be tuned and time-stretched. Filters, gates, and envelopes can be applied. Each drum has volume, pan, and two sends. Click on a drum to edit the parameters for that specific drum.

Figure 6.6

PolySynth

PolySynth is a model of the original Roland Juno synthesizer series. The Juno series was notable because it used analog oscillators to make sound, but unlike older synths such as the MiniMoog, the oscillators were under digital control. Also unlike the MiniMoog, the Juno synthesizers were polyphonic.

Classic PolySynth sounds include synthesizer brass and strings PolySynth also provides bass, organ, and electric piano sounds.

Modulo

Modulo is a subtractive synthesizer that uses two oscillators to create sound. Each oscillator can use a wide range of waveforms.

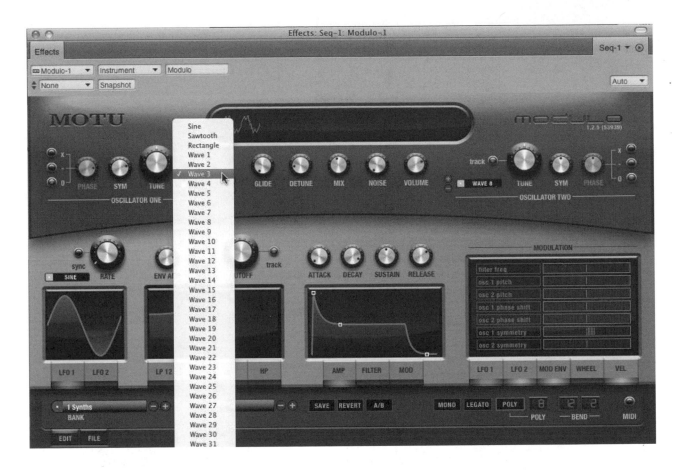

Figure 6.7

Modulo gets its name from its ability to modulate parameters using LFOs and external MIDI controllers. Right-click on a parameter in the Modulation window to get the MIDI Learn window.

Right-click on in the Modulation window to assign an external MIDI controller or internal modulator to the parameter.

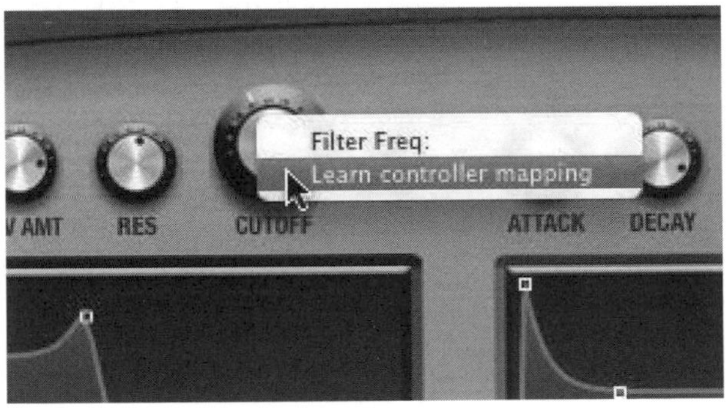

Figure 6.8

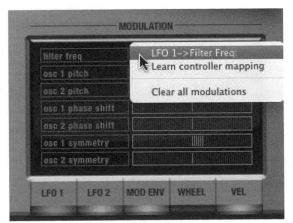

Modulo uses its own internal patch management system. Patches are organized into banks. Select a bank and then select patches from within that bank.

Figure 6.9

Figure 6.10

Proton

Proton is an FM (a frequency modulation) synthesizer. Proton uses two oscillators to make sound. The first oscillator is called the *carrier*, and this produces the audio output of Proton. The second oscillator is called a *modulator*. The modulator works to alter the waveshape of the carrier.

FM synthesis sounds very different from subtractive synthesis. FM sounds have a bell-like quality.

The display in the middle of the Proton window can be switched to show the output waveform. This provides a visual understanding of how the sound is being created.

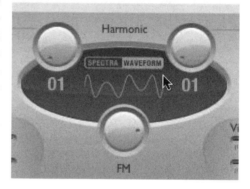

Figure 6.11

Nanosampler

Nanosampler is a one-shot sample player. That means a single sample can be loaded and triggered. Samples can be loaded as presets. Audio files in WAV and AIF formats can be dragged directly onto the Nanosampler interface. New samples can be stored with the project or in a user library.

Nanosampler can be used to play back any type of instrument sample. Nanosampler can also be useful for triggering sound effects.

Nanosampler provides basic sample-editing tools. Sample start and end times can be edited. Samples can be looped. Samples can be modulated with envelopes, filters, and LFOs.

Figure 6.12

Instrument Tracks

In Digital Performer, virtual instrument plug-ins run as inserts on instrument tracks. Unless the virtual instrument is self-triggering, at least one MIDI track is used in combination with the instrument track.

To add an instrument track in Digital Performer, go to the Project menu and choose Add Track > Instrument Track. Under this menu the stock instruments that ship with Digital Performer are listed, along with any installed third-party instruments.

If one of the listed instruments is selected, Digital Performer will create a new instrument track, and the instrument will be created within an insert on that track.

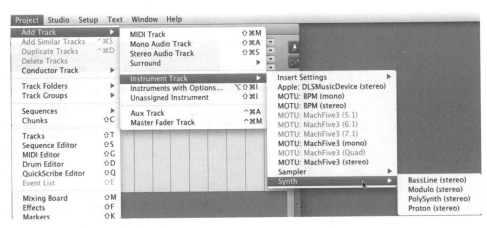

Figure 6.13

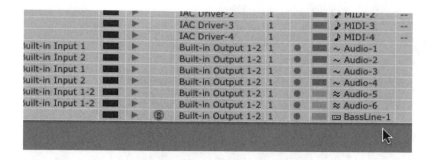

Figure 6.14

Creating a MIDI Track to Trigger the Instrument Track

In order to trigger the virtual instrument, at least one MIDI track is required in addition to the instrument track. The MIDI track can be used to pass a live MIDI signal from outside the computer through to the instrument track. To pass external MIDI through a MIDI track to the instrument track, the MIDI track must be record-enabled.

Assigning the output of a MIDI track to an instrument is done at the output of the MIDI track. Once a virtual instrument has been created in Digital Performer, it becomes an available output destination for any MIDI track.

Once MIDI is recorded in the MIDI track, that MIDI can be played back to trigger the instrument. The only information that can be recorded into an instrument track is automation for the instrument and any effects plug-ins that may be inserted after the instrument.

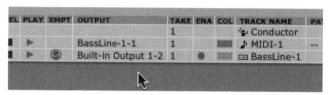

Figure 6.15

Creating a MIDI Track and Instrument Track with a Single Operation

It is possible to create an instrument track and a preassigned MIDI track with a single operation. Go to the Project menu and choose Add Track > Instruments With Options. A dialog box will open that allows the creation of multiple instrument tracks, as well as preassigned MIDI tracks.

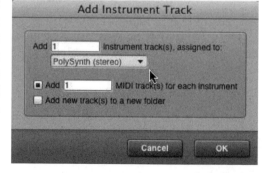

Figure 6.16

Audio Routing

An instrument track has an audio output. The audio output of the instrument track is mixed in with the outputs of other audio tracks and aux tracks. Audio output of an instrument track can be processed or recorded like any other audio signal inside Digital Performer.

Some virtual instruments allow audio signal to be routed to separate outputs from the instrument track. For example, a virtual instrument that is used to play back drum sounds may allow for the individual drums to be routed to separate audio outputs for independent processing. The separate outputs from the instrument show up as inputs to audio tracks or aux tracks.

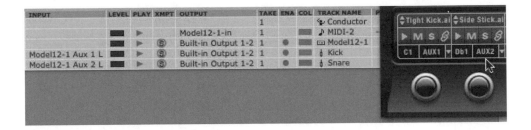

Figure 6.17

Presets and Patch Lists

Presets patches or sounds are an important part of using virtual instruments. Most virtual instruments ship with presets. In some cases the user can customize or create new sounds that can be saved as additional presets.

Instrument Presets

Some virtual instruments have their own internal preset management system. Other instruments may rely on Digital Performer to manage presets. Digital Performer can store instrument presets, regardless of whether the instrument has its own preset management system.

Every instrument plug-in has a preset menu. The preset menu lists any current presets and provides the ability to save new presets.

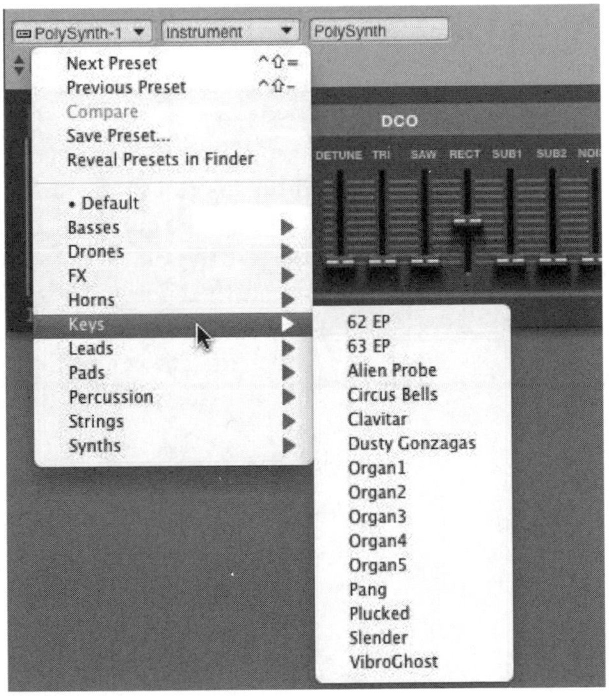

Multitimbral Instruments

A multitimbral instrument is an instrument that contains multiple independent instruments. Each separate instrument is typically accessed using different MIDI channels. For example, a multitimbral instrument could host a violin, viola, cello, and contrabass. Each instrument can be set to receive on a different MIDI channel. Separate MIDI tracks can then be created with different channel outputs to the same multitimbral instrument. That allows each MIDI track to trigger a different instrument within the multitimbral instrument.

Multitimbral instruments typically provide routing so that the individual instruments within the multitimbral instrument can be processed and recorded separately.

Creating Audio Files

Digital Performer can convert the output of a virtual instrument track into an audio file. The audio will be

Figure 6.18

placed in a newly created audio track. To do this, select both the instrument track and the MIDI track that is triggering the instrument. The region that is selected is what will be printed to audio. Therefore, if the instrument plays the entire length of the sequence, make sure that the selection of the MIDI and instrument tracks extend for the entire sequence.

Freeze-Selected Tracks

Once the instrument track and associated MIDI tracks are selected, go to the Audio menu and choose Freeze Selected Tracks. This will cause Digital Performer to create a new audio track and to record the output of the virtual instrument into that track. If the output of the instrument track is stereo, a stereo audio track will be created with the Freeze function. To freeze to a mono audio track, change the output of the instrument track to a mono output before freezing.

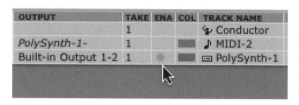

OUTPUT	TAKE	ENA	COL	TRACK NAME
	1			🎚 Conductor
PolySynth-1-	1		▉	♪ MIDI-2
Built-in Output 1-2	1	●	▉	▭ PolySynth-1

Figure 6.19

Once a virtual instrument audio output has been recorded into an audio track, the original virtual instrument can be deleted from the sequence to free up CPU power and RAM. However, it's also possible to temporarily disable the instrument so that it is still in the sequence but not using CPU or RAM resources. This allows the composer to come back to the MIDI track and instrument track and make changes later if desired. To temporarily disable the instrument track, deselect the ENA button for the instrument track in the Tracks window.

Recording into Audio Tracks

It is possible to route audio outputs from a virtual instrument into audio tracks via buses. The output of an instrument track can be assigned to a mono, stereo, or surround bus, which can then be used to send signal into a mono, stereo, or surround audio track. The output of the instrument can then be recorded into the audio track. Essentially, the Freeze function automates this process.

Manually setting up audio tracks to record virtual instruments is useful when the instrument has additional outputs that are routed to buses. For example, the Model 12 drum instrument included with Digital Performer allows each drum sound to be sent to a separate output. Perhaps the cymbals and toms will be mixed and sent directly to the instrument track output. Perhaps the kick and snare sounds can be sent to separate outputs via buses. Those buses could be routed to audio tracks. That would allow the kick and snare sounds to be recorded and processed separately from the rest of the drum kit. The cymbals and toms could be printed to audio via the Freeze function, or by manually patching the output of the instrument track to a bus and audio track.

Live Performance

Many musicians are now using computers and virtual instruments to replace hardware musical instruments onstage. A computer equipped with virtual instruments can create any sound. This means that the musician no longer needs to carry around large amounts of gear to get those sounds.

A typical live-performance setup consists of a computer, an audio interface, and an external MIDI controller such as keyboard or drum pads. The MIDI controller sends MIDI into the computer to trigger virtual instruments. The virtual instruments generate sound that is routed out the audio interface to the stage monitors and front-of-house speakers.

Some virtual instruments can run as stand-alone applications. It is also possible to use Digital Performer as a host for virtual instruments in a live-performance setup. Running virtual instruments inside Digital Performer provides additional functions that a stand-alone instrument cannot match.

Digital Performer can host multiple instrument plug-ins at the same time. Instrument plug-ins can be processed with effects plug-ins. The Digital Performer mixer provides a way to control and monitor output levels of instruments. While hosting virtual instruments, Digital Performer can also play back sequences and video files, as well as process external audio signals.

Chapter 7
MIXING, EFFECTS, AND AUTOMATION

This chapter describes how to set up and control the basic mix of a MIDI and audio sequence, and how to work with signal routing and effects processing. It also describes how to mix and master a Digital Performer project.

Digital Performer provides powerful and comprehensive tools for mixing and processing audio and MIDI signals, and ships with a long list of professional-quality effects plug-ins. This chapter will discuss how and where to use MIDI and audio effects.

Every aspect of a mix can be automated. It is possible to create multiple mix takes. Automation can be created and edited for all aspects of a mix.

Digital Performer includes the Mixing Board window, which resembles a hardware mixing board. The purpose of the Mixing Board window is to facilitate volume and pan control for audio and MIDI tracks and virtual instrument tracks. The Mixing Board window is where effects plug-ins are set up to process audio and MIDI signals.

Digital Performer provides powerful and comprehensive signal routing functions for audio and MIDI. It is possible to create audio subgroups, effects sends and returns, and master faders. Signal routing can be set up and modified in a number of different windows.

The Mixing Board Window

The Mixing Board window is used to display fader strips for sequence tracks. Any combination of track fader strips can be shown or hidden. The interface of the Mixing Board window is completely customizable, and multiple board layouts can be saved and recalled.

Audio and MIDI signal routing can be set up and controlled from the Mixing Board window. Instrument and effects plug-ins are set up and controlled from the Mixing Board window.

Mix automation can be created and edited from the Mixing Board window. It is possible to save and recall multiple mix takes in the Mixing Board window.

Figure 7.1

Figure 7.2

The Mixing Board window can be opened from a tab in the Consolidated window or from the Project menu. It can be opened via key command, MIDI remote command, or shortcut button. The default key command to open the Mixing Board window is Shift + M.

Hide and Show Tracks

The Track Selector is used to show or hide any combination of tracks within the Mixing Board window. If a track is selected in an edit window and the Mixing Board window is then opened, the Mixing Board window will display the track or tracks that were selected in the edit window. It is also possible to save configurations of visible tracks with the Mixing Board's various board layouts. Board layouts are saved and recalled from the Mixing Board window minimenu.

Track Order

The order of the tracks in the Mixing Board window is initially determined by the track order in the Tracks window. This preference can be disabled by unchecking Lock Layout to Track Order in the Mixing Board window minimenu.

Tracks can be dragged left or right in the Mixing Board window by clicking on the very bottom of the fader strip.

Display Mixing Board Window Sections

The Mixing Board window contains fader strips. Fader strips can have many options that can be shown or hidden. The sections of the Mixing Board window can be selected for display in the minimenu.

When a pan control is used with a mono audio track, the panner will move the mono signal between the two channels of assigned output. When a pan control is used with a stereo audio track, the pan control will attenuate the left or right side of the stereo signal.

For independent control of left and right signals within a stereo audio track, insert the Trim plug-in on the track.

Audio Volume and Pan

The volume fader on an audio track, aux track, instrument track, or master fader controls the audio gain of the output of the track. In Digital Performer, when an audio fader is set to 0 VU, the fader is not attenuating or boosting the signal. This is called *unity gain*. Double-click on a fader to make it jump to 0 VU. Audio faders in the Digital Performer Mixing Board window provide 6 dB of available boost for the audio signal. Additional gain can be added to the audio signal with a Trim plug-in.

An audio panner exists in the Mixing Board window if an audio track has two or more channels of audio output. If an audio track is assigned to a mono output, it has no pan control. If an audio track is assigned to a stereo output, a stereo panner is automatically assigned to the track. If an audio track is assigned to more than two channels of output, a surround panner is automatically assigned to the track output.

MIDI Volume and Pan

The volume faders in the Mixing Board window for MIDI tracks generate MIDI CC 7 data. MIDI continuous controller number 7 is typically used to control the volume of a MIDI device. Most hardware MIDI modules and software virtual instruments respond to CC 7 data.

The pan controls for MIDI tracks in the Mixing Board window generate MIDI CC 10. MIDI CC 10 is typically used to control the pan output of a MIDI device that has stereo output.

It is important to understand that MIDI is not sound. The fader and pan controls for a MIDI track in Digital Performer do not control audio volume or panning. These controls send data to the assigned output of the MIDI track. Therefore, it is up to whatever hardware or software is receiving that data to respond correctly.

Attach MIDI Controller

The faders and pan controls of the Mixing Board window can be mapped to remote MIDI controllers. That allows remote control of the basic mix functions from any hardware device that has a knob or slider that generates MIDI controller commands. To map an external slider or knob to a fader or panner in the Mixing Board window, go to the minimenu and select Attach MIDI Controller. Click on a fader or panner in the Mixing Board window. The fader or panner will be highlighted with a flashing red border. Move the slider or knob on the external MIDI controller. The highlighted fader or panner will learn the MIDI command and will animate when the external controller is moved. Click on another fader or panner to assign more controllers, or press Return to exit the assign mode.

The Meter Bridge Window

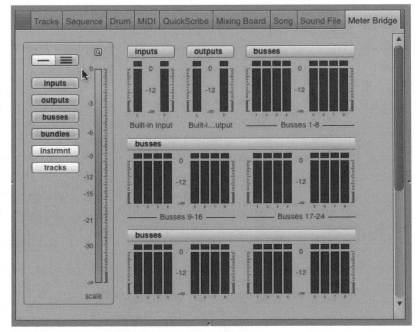

Digital Performer provides a dedicated window for audio VU meters. The Meter Bridge can be opened in the Consolidated window with a tab. It can be opened via shortcut or MIDI command, or from the Studio menu. The default key command to open the Meter Bridge is Shift + Z.

The Meter Bridge includes buttons to show or hide audio inputs, outputs, buses, and tracks. There are also meters for audio bundles and instrument track outputs.

Meter width is adjustable via the Magnifying Glass button on the left. Meters can also be displayed in a single row or in multiple rows.

Figure 7.3

The Channel Strip Window

The Channel Strip window displays the mix controls for a single track. This can be useful if it is desirable to display the controls for a single track separately from the Mixing Board window.

The Channel Strip window can be opened in a sidebar of the Consolidated window or as an independent window. The Channel Strip window can be opened from the Studio menu. There is no default key command to open the Channel Strip window. A key command or MIDI remote command can be set in the Commands window.

Like the Mixer, the Channel Strip window can hide or show different sections via its minimenu. Unlike the Mixing Board window, the Channel Strip window can be set to show its contents in columns.

Figure 7.4

The Channel Strip window will change to display the mix functions for any track selected in an editing window. In the bottom right-hand corner of the window is a Lock button. The button will lock the currently visible track to the Channel Strip window, so that if other tracks are selected, the Channel Strip continues to display the locked track.

MIDI Routing

As with audio, MIDI data follows a signal path. The following section describes MIDI routing in Digital Performer. This includes MIDI input and output to the software, as well as patching of MIDI signals within the software.

MIDI Monitor

When external MIDI data reaches Digital Performer, the first place the data goes is to the MIDI Monitor window. The MIDI Monitor window displays all MIDI inputs to Digital Performer, including the specific MIDI channels for each input. The MIDI monitor is a diagnostic tool to check that MIDI is reaching Digital Performer.

The MIDI Monitor window can be opened in a sidebar of the Consolidated window. It can be opened via shortcut button or from the Studio menu. The default key command to open the MIDI Monitor window is Shift + W.

Signal Flow

By default, Digital Performer is in Omni Receive mode for MIDI. This means that by record-enabling a MIDI track, the track will accept data from any MIDI source, on any MIDI channel. In Omni Receive mode, no input is specified for a record-enabled MIDI track. In Omni Receive mode, only one MIDI track can be record-enabled at a time.

If there are multiple external MIDI input signals that need to be simultaneously routed to different MIDI tracks, engage Multi-Record mode from the Studio menu. When Multi-Record is engaged, it is possible to record-enable more than one MIDI track at a time. In Multi-Record mode, the specific input for each MIDI track must be assigned.

If a MIDI command is currently mapped to a remote control or attached to a fader or panner in the Mixing Board window, it is filtered so that it cannot be recorded into a MIDI track.

Record-enabling a MIDI track patches MIDI input to output through that track. That allows the composer to record-enable a MIDI track and hear the correct instrument when playing on an external MIDI controller. By default, Digital Performer rechannelizes the incoming MIDI data to the channel specified by the output of the MIDI track.

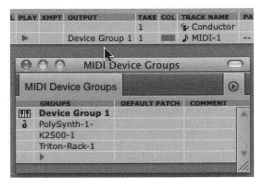

The output of a MIDI track can be assigned to external MIDI hardware or to internal virtual instruments. On Mac, MIDI tracks can be assigned to the network driver or the IAC driver of the Apple Audio MIDI Setup. On Windows, there are third-party utilities available that provide for MIDI routing within the OS. If a ReWire application is running alongside Digital Performer, MIDI track outputs will include the ReWire destinations.

A MIDI track can be assigned to multiple outputs by way of a *device group*. Select New Device Group as the output for a MIDI track. The Device Group window will open, allowing multiple MIDI output destinations to be selected.

Figure 7.5

Virtual Instrument Plug-ins

Virtual instrument plug-ins are hosted on instrument tracks. An instrument track accepts MIDI input and generates audio output. No assignment is made in the input field of an instrument track. MIDI is sent into an instrument track by assigning the output from one or more MIDI tracks to the virtual instrument running inside in the instrument track. MIDI and audio data does not get recorded to an instrument track. The only information that can be recorded in an instrument track is automation data for the track and plug-ins.

It is possible to assign the outputs of multiple MIDI tracks to the same virtual instrument. If the virtual instrument is multitimbral, it may use different MIDI channel assignments to access the different sounds within the instrument. For example, the following figure shows a picture of MOTU's MachFive 3 sampler running inside Digital Performer as an instrument plug-in. In the picture, MachFive 3 is being used to host four separate sounds for a string quartet. Each sound is assigned to a different incoming MIDI channel. Four MIDI tracks with separate output assignments are used to trigger the four stringed instruments within MachFive 3.

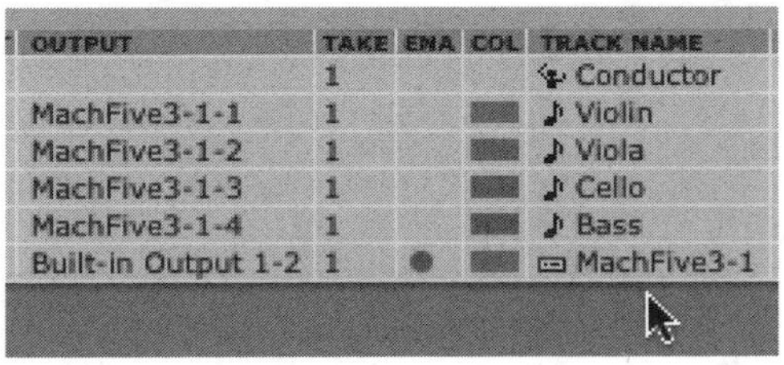

OUTPUT	TAKE	ENA	COL	TRACK NAME
	1			♪ Conductor
MachFive3-1-1	1			♪ Violin
MachFive3-1-2	1			♪ Viola
MachFive3-1-3	1			♪ Cello
MachFive3-1-4	1			♪ Bass
Built-in Output 1-2	1	●		▭ MachFive3-1

Figure 7.6

A virtual instrument plug-in is assigned to the topmost insert of the instrument track in the Mixing Board window. Additional inserts below the instrument can be used for audio effects plug-ins to further process the audio output of the instrument.

The output of an instrument track is an audio signal that is mixed with other audio signals. By default, an instrument track has a stereo output. Some virtual instruments allow for multiple audio outputs. If the virtual instrument allows for additional outputs, those outputs will be available as buses within Digital Performer, and will show up as available inputs for audio tracks and aux tracks.

Figure 7.7

Sidechain Routing

Some plug-ins can accept a MIDI signal through a sidechain input. For example, the MW Gate is an audio effects plug-in that can be triggered via MIDI notes. Put the MW Gate on a bass guitar audio track. Trigger the gate with a MIDI kick drum track. Now the bass is heard only when the kick drum triggers the gate. If a plug-in with sidechain routing is available in the mix, that sidechain input becomes an available output destination for MIDI tracks.

Figure 7.8

Audio Routing

Digital Performer provides comprehensive audio routing functions. Audio signals can be recorded, played, and monitored through audio tracks. Audio signals can be routed and processed through aux tracks and master faders. Buses can be used as internal patch cords to pass audio signals and create subgroups and effects sends.

Track Inputs and Outputs

Click on the input or output field of an audio track or aux track to see the currently available audio inputs and outputs. The input and output fields will display audio inputs and outputs that are currently configured in the Bundles window. The input and output fields will also display the option to configure new input and output bundles.

If an audio input or output is not configured and visible in the input or output list, click on New Mono Bundle or New Stereo Bundle. This will display a list of all possible audio inputs or outputs for the track. The list will include inputs and outputs from the currently assigned audio interface, as well as internal buses. Any available virtual instrument aux outputs will also be available to audio track and aux track inputs.

Aux Tracks

The word "aux" is short for "auxiliary." Aux tracks are used to pass audio signals. Aux tracks do not record or play audio. Aux tracks are typically used to create subgroups and effects returns. Aux tracks can be used to pass external audio signals through Digital Performer. Aux tracks can be used to monitor additional outputs from virtual instruments.

Aux tracks have sends and effects inserts. Aux track parameters can be automated, including volume, pan, sends, and plug-in effects.

Buses

A bus is a virtual audio patch cord inside Digital Performer. Buses are used to route audio signals between audio tracks, aux tracks, and virtual instruments. Buses are used for audio sidechain routing. Buses are used for effects sends. Buses are often used in combination with aux tracks to create subgroups within a mix.

Subgroups

Creating a subgroup is a way of routing multiple audio signals through a single fader. For example, a drum set may get recorded to separate audio tracks. Those audio tracks can then be routed through a single stereo aux track so that the aux track provides a single volume fader for just the drums.

To set up a drum subgroup, do the following:

- Add an aux track from the Project menu.
- Set the output of the aux track to the main monitor outputs.
- For the input of the aux tracks, select New Stereo Bundle > Bus 1–2. If buses 1–2 are already in use somewhere else in the mix, select an unused bus pair.
- Set the outputs of the drum audio tracks to the bus pair. The drum audio tracks now send their signals into the bus pair, which routes that stereo signal to the input of the audio track. The aux track passes the combined drum track signals to the main monitor outputs.
- Name the aux track "Drum Sub."

Now the entire drum set mix can be controlled with a single fader. The aux track also provides a way to put effects plug-ins on the combined signal passing through. For example, an EQ on the Drum Sub aux track will affect the entire drum set.

Sends

Sends provide ways to pass audio from an audio track to an alternate destination. Sends are typically used for additional monitor mixes and to route audio signals to effects returns. Sends can also be used to generate audio sidechain signals.

By default, audio tracks, aux tracks, and master faders in Digital Performer have four available sends. Up to 20 sends can be created and displayed via Set Number Of Sends in the Mixing Board window minimenu.

Each send has four parameters, a volume control, a Mute button, and a pop-up menu to assign its output. Sends can be assigned to buses or directly to audio interface outputs. Sends can also be set as prefader or postfader. Prefader sends are typically used for secondary monitor mixes. Postfader sends are typically used for effects sends.

In the following figure, an audio track named Vocal has a send assigned to a bus. The bus has been renamed as Verb Bus in the Bundles window. The Verb Bus is assigned to the input of an aux track named Verb Return. A ProVerb plug-in is assigned to an insert of the aux track. When the send on the track named Vocal is turned up, signal is sent through the Verb Bus into the aux track, which passes the signal through the ProVerb plug-in.

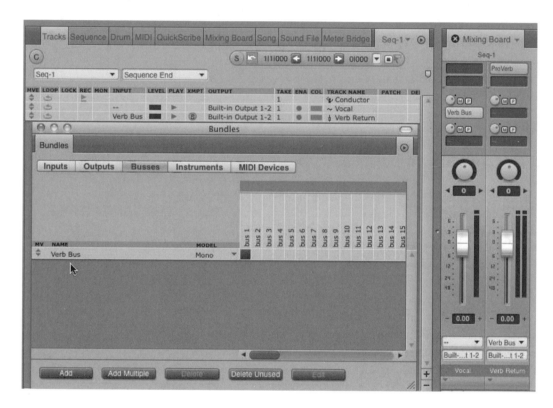

Figure 7.9

Master Faders

Master faders are very similar to aux tracks. The difference between an aux track and master fader is that an aux track can have separate audio inputs and outputs. Master faders do not have assignable inputs. Master faders exist on the outputs of buses or audio outputs.

It is a good idea to always use a master fader on the main monitor output of a mix. The master fader provides a way to monitor and control the volume of the overall mix. Master faders have effects inserts, which allow plug-ins to be placed on the final output of the mix. For example, it is typical to put a limiter on the last insert of a master fader to ensure that output volume never clips.

It is possible to have multiple master faders in a mix. For example, master faders can be used on separate monitor mixes as well as on the main monitor mix. In the following figure, there are four audio tracks that are routed through a master fader to the main monitor output. There is also a second master fader that controls the combined outputs of the sends of the audio tracks for a secondary monitor mix that is routed to a different set of outputs on the audio interface.

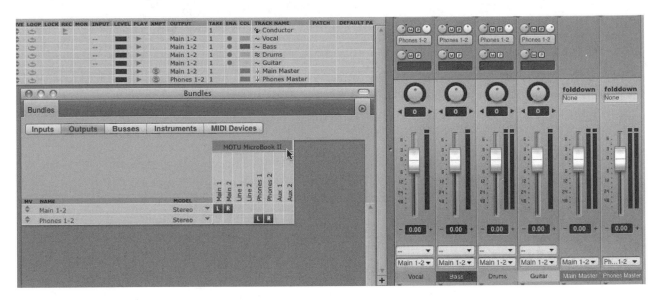

Figure 7.10

Monitor Mixes

For a simple setup, a single stereo or surround output from Digital Performer is all that is required for audio monitoring. In some situations, multiple monitor output mixes are required. For example, if an ensemble is recording and the musicians are using headphones, each musician may request a separate mix. Each headphone mix will require a separate mix within Digital Performer. The separate mixes will be sent out through separate outputs of the audio interface to headphones for the musicians.

If the same main mix needs to be sent to multiple output destinations, assign all audio outputs to a bus pair. Create aux tracks for each set of outputs. Assign the outputs of the aux tracks to the separate external outputs. Assign the bus pair as the input for each of the aux tracks. Each aux track passes the same stereo mix to a different set of outputs.

Figure 7.11

If different mixes are required for the separate monitor outputs, use sends from the audio tracks to create those mixes. Assign a send from each audio track to a single mono or stereo output on the audio interface. Monitor mix sends are usually set to prefader so that changes to the fader for the main track output do not affect the secondary monitor mixes.

Effects Plug-ins

Digital Performer ships with a full complement of high-quality audio and MIDI effects plug-ins. Digital Performer also supports plug-ins made by other companies. Instrument and effects plug-ins work in specific formats. On the Mac, Digital Performer supports MAS, Audio Unit, and VST plug-in formats. On Windows, Digital Performer supports MAS and VST formats.

Effects plug-ins can be used nondestructively to process a live signal or track playback signal. Effects plug-ins can also be used to print an effect to an audio file. The stock Digital Performer plug-ins are listed and individually described under the Help menu. Check the Digital Performer Plug-Ins Guide under the Help menu.

Inserts

Audio and MIDI plug-ins are applied to tracks in the Mixing Board window via inserts. Inserts can be shown or hidden in the Mixing Board window by selecting or deselecting Inserts in the Mixing Board minimenu. When inserts are visible, they are displayed at the top of the fader strip.

By default, a new sequence in Digital Performer has five inserts per track. The number of available inserts can be changed by selecting Set Number Of Effect Inserts from the Mixing Board window minimenu. Up to 20 inserts per track can be configured.

Signal flows from top to bottom through inserts. By default, inserts are before the fader in the signal path. It is possible to make the lower inserts postfader by dragging the divider at the bottom the insert list up. Inserts below the divider will be postfader.

Click on an insert to add a plug-in effect to a track. MIDI track inserts will show a list of available MIDI effects.

Figure 7.12

Click on an audio track insert to display a window that lists all available audio effects plug-ins.

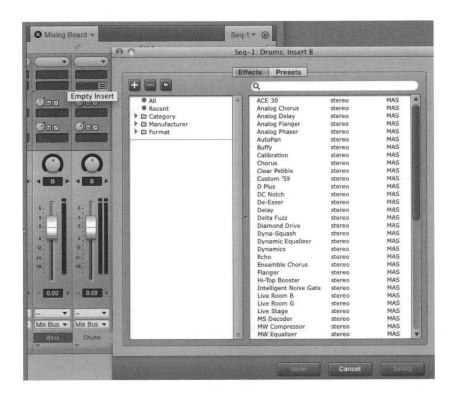

Figure 7.13

The Effect Chooser window provides a search field, as well as the ability to view plug-ins based on manufacturer or category. It is also possible to select effects plug-ins based on presets. Choose an effect or preset to add it to the track insert.

When a plug-in is added to an effects insert, the plug-in window will open. If the plug-in window is closed, it can be reopened by double-clicking on the plug-in name in the insert.

To delete a plug-in from an insert, select the plug-in in the insert and press the Delete key. Shift-click to select multiple plug-ins.

Plug-ins can be dragged up or down in the insert list to change their order in the signal path. Hold down the Command key and click-and-drag the plug-in insert up or down. Plug-ins can be copied from one insert to another, including copying to inserts on other tracks. Press Command + Option-click-and-drag to copy a plug-in from one insert to another. Multiple plug-ins can be copied with a single operation by Shift-clicking to select the plug-ins, and then pressing Command + Option-clicking-and-dragging to copy.

At the top of the insert list is an Insert Settings menu that contains effects presets. These presets can include chains of multiple plug-in effects. It is possible to store and save effects presets in the Insert Settings menu.

MIDI Plug-ins

Digital Performer ships with MIDI plug-ins. MIDI plug-ins are inserted on MIDI tracks. MIDI plug-ins process MIDI data as it passes through the MIDI track.

MIDI plug-ins change MIDI data. For example, the Echo plug-in works by generating additional MIDI notes based on MIDI input. The Arpeggiator plug-in also generates additional MIDI notes.

Some MIDI plug-ins work only with playback of prerecorded MIDI tracks. For example, the Quantize plug-in cannot process MIDI data as it is being played live. The quantize plug-in works only when playing back prerecorded MIDI data.

Using MIDI plug-ins is an excellent way of processing MIDI playback without altering the actual data in the track. However, there may be times that it is desirable to print the MIDI plug-in effect to the track. For example, the Quantize plug-in could be used on play back to experiment with different settings in real time. When the ideal quantization values are determined, that quantization can be printed to the MIDI track. To print MIDI effects plug-ins, chose a region of one or more MIDI tracks and choose Capture Real Time MIDI Effects from the Region menu.

Audio Effects Plug-ins

Audio effects plug-ins are used to process an audio signal. Typical audio effects include EQ, compression, and reverb. There are many ways to process audio signals, including special effects such as phase shifters and delays. Some plug-ins can take a mono input signal and generate a stereo output signal.

When an audio effects plug-in is inserted on an audio track, an aux track, an instrument track, or a master fader, it processes the audio signal in real time as that signal passes through. Effects plug-ins can be added, deleted, changed, or automated at any time.

There are three typical places in an audio signal chain to use effects plug-ins. If a plug-in is placed on the insert of an audio track or instrument track, it affects only the audio output of that track. If a plug-in is inserted on an aux track or master fader track, it affects all audio passing through that aux or master fader track. The third way to use plug-in effects is within a send and return set up.

It is possible to print effects plug-ins to sound files. There are two ways to do this. If there are effects in inserts on an audio track, select a region of the track—or multiple tracks—and choose Freeze Selected Tracks from the Audio menu. This will record the selected audio tracks into newly created audio tracks, and therefore print the plug-in effects from the original tracks to the audio in the new tracks. The second method of printing an audio plug-in effect to a soundbite is to select the soundbite and then go to Audio > Apply Plug-In. A submenu will be displayed that lists all plug-ins. Choose a plug-in, and its window will open, where there will be a Preview button to audition the effect, and an Apply button to print the effect.

Sends and Returns

Using an effects send or return is a way to use a single plug-in and send varying amounts of different tracks through it. A typical use of an effects send or return is to have a single reverb plug-in that can be used by multiple tracks.

Sends can be shown or hidden in the Mixing Board window by selecting or deselecting Sends in the Mixing Board minimenu. When sends are visible they are displayed above the panner and automation controls in the fader strip.

The default new file template opens with two sends per audio track and aux track. The number of available sends can be changed via selecting Set Number Of Sends from the Mixing Board window minimenu. Up to 20 sends per track can be configured.

Each send provides a volume control. If the send is assigned to a stereo destination, a pan knob will be available. Each send has a Mute button. Each send has a pre/post button. By default, sends are set to postfader. This means that if the volume fader is turned down, that will also attenuate the signal going to the send. This is typical for an effects send. Typically, a send is set to prefader when it is being used to create a secondary monitor mix.

Sends can be assigned to outputs on the audio interface, or to internal buses. To set up a send and return for a plug-in in Digital Performer, do the following:

- Assign the send to a bus. For most plug-ins, a mono bus is appropriate. Click on the pop-up menu for the send and choose New Mono Bundle > Bus 1. If bus 1 is already in use somewhere else in the mix, choose a bus that is not being used.
- Create an aux track. Go to the Project menu and choose Add Track > Aux Track.
- Assign the bus as the input for the aux track.
- Assign the output of the bus track to the main monitor outputs.
- Add an effects plug-in to an insert on the aux track. In the case of a plug-in such as a reverb, set the effects mix control to 100% wet.

Now when the send for a track is turned up, the signal will be sent through the aux track and the reverb, and will be mixed with the original signal from the audio track.

Effects on Subgroups

It is possible to run multiple tracks through a common set of plug-ins. For example, if a drum set was recorded with separate microphones, there could be separate audio tracks for kick drum, snare, toms, and overhead mics. If a plug-in is placed on the insert of any of those tracks, that plug-in will affect only the one track.

Aux tracks are used to create subgroups. If a plug-in is placed on an insert of the aux track, the plug-in will affect all the signals going through the subgroup.

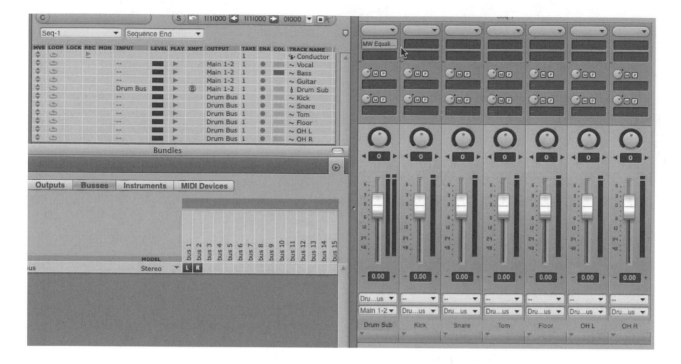

Figure 7.14

Effects on a Master Fader

Master faders are typically used on the final output of a mix. If a plug-in is assigned to an insert on a master fader, the entire mix goes through that plug-in. It is typical to put an EQ and limiter plug-ins on the inserts of a master fader.

Automation

Automation is the process of controlling a mix parameter over time, via events embedded in a track. All aspects of a Digital Performer mix can be automated, including individual effects parameters.

There are several ways to create and edit automation in Digital Performer. If an external control surface is connected to the computer, then that can be used to control automation. Once automation information is created, it can be temporarily disabled if needed.

Recording Automation

The most direct way to record automation information is to manually move a control while Digital Performer is in Automation Record mode. Automation Record can be enabled for any track from within the Mixing Board window.

Figure 7.15

Automation can be enabled for any visible track in the Sequence Editor window.

Figure 7.16

Automation Record can also be enabled from inside any plug-in window.

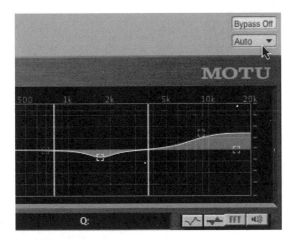

Figure 7.17

Enable Automation Record mode for a track and play the sequence. There is no need to press the Record button in the Control Panel. Move any mix or plug-in parameter for the track. Stop the sequence. Rewind and play. The parameter will play back the automated move.

Disable Automation

It is important to understand that initially, there is no automation information for any parameter for any track in a new Digital Performer sequence. This means that any mix parameter can be changed, and that parameter won't change again until the next time it is adjusted.

Once the automation data has been created for a mix parameter, the parameter will follow the automation. It is possible to disable automation for a track. This is done with the Automation Play control, which is found next to the Automation Record control in the Mixing Board, Sequence Editor, and Plug-in windows.

Creating Automation in the Sequence Editor Window

Automation can be created by clicking in a track in the Sequence Editor window. On the left edge of each track in the Sequence Editor is an Insert pop-up menu. Click on the Insert menu and select the type of automation to be added. Click, or click-and-drag in the track to add automation data.

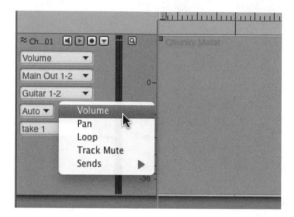

Figure 7.18

Editing Automation

There are three ways to edit existing automation data. If the track is in Automation Record mode, adjusting a mix parameter while the sequence plays will overwrite the automation data in the track. Automation can be graphically edited in the Sequence Editor window, or in any other editor window that displays automation. Automation can be edited by selecting a region of data and choosing Change Continuous Data from the Region menu.

In the Sequence Editor window, automation for audio tracks displays as a continuous line from left to right. The horizontal position of the line indicates the current value of the automated parameter.

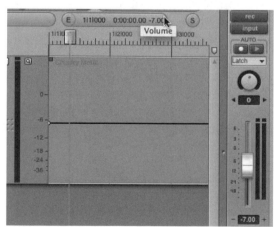

Figure 7.19

Click with the mouse to add points to the line.

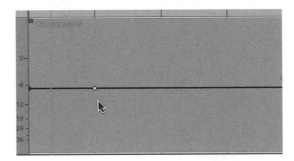

Figure 7.20

Drag points up or down to change automation values.

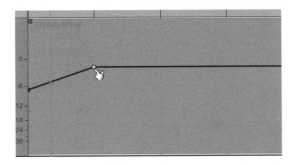

Figure 7.21

Click to select an automation point and press the Delete key to delete the automation point.

Use the Reshape tool from the Tool palette to redraw automation with preset curves and lines. If the Edit Resolution button is engaged, the Reshape tool will draw while snapping to the assigned resolution.

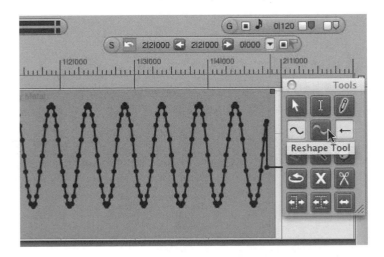

Figure 7.22

Select multiple automation by clicking-and-dragging over those points. Move one automation point, and all selected automation points move together.

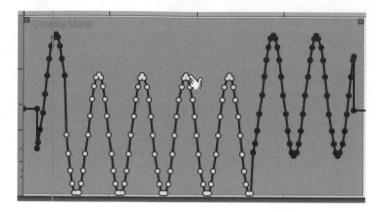

Figure 7.23

If automation is enabled, the automation line will display as a solid line. If automation is disabled for the track, automation lines are displayed as dotted lines.

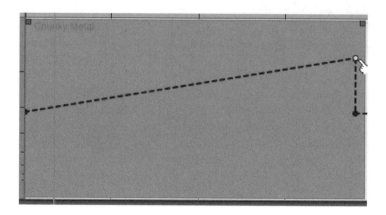

Figure 7.24

To scale automation for a track or multiple tracks, select those tracks and the desired time range and choose Change Continuous Data from the Region menu. Select the type of automation to be changed and use the options to make that change. For example, to scale the audio automation volume of a mix up or down, select Audio Volume and choose the option to Scale To % Of Current Value. A scale value of 70% will attenuate all automation volume data by 30%.

Chapter **8**
WORKING WITH MOVIES

Digital Performer can open and play back a digital movie file. The movie file is linked to the transport and timeline of the sequence. This allows Digital Performer to be used to compose music and create soundtracks for movies.

When the soundtrack is completed, Digital Performer can create a new movie file that contains the audio from the sequence. Digital Performer is not a video-editing program. However, when bouncing to a new movie file, Digital Performer can trim the beginning and the end of the original movie to make it shorter. Digital Performer can also add video black at the beginning or end of the new movie to add space.

Opening a Movie

Open a movie by choosing Movie from the Project menu. A dialog box will open that allows a movie to be selected from any connected hard drive.

Digital Performer can open and play most digital movie files that can be played on the computer desktop. In some cases a specific movie format may be required if the movie is to be played out through an external video interface. If a movie file is not recognized by Digital Performer, it is usually possible to convert that file to a readable format with some sort of video conversion utility.

Very large movie files can use a significant amount of computer power to play back. An optimized computer setup typically uses a dedicated hard drive for movie playback for maximum efficiency.

Right-click on the Movie window to get the minimenu. When the Movie window is displayed in a sidebar of the Consolidated window, there is a dedicated tab for the minimenu.

Movie Playback

By default, a newly opened movie starts at the beginning of the sequence timeline and is linked to the transport controls. When the sequence plays, the movie plays.

A movie can be opened in a sidebar of the Consolidated window or as an independent window. Double-click on the movie to pop it in or out of the sidebar. When the movie is displayed in its own window, that window can be expanded to take up the entire computer screen. If multiple monitors are connected to the computer, the movie can be placed on any monitor.

A movie can also be directed to play out through an external converter to a dedicated video monitor or video recorder.

Movie Audio

By default, a soundtrack in the movie will be routed to the first available stereo outputs in the Bundles window. Movie soundtrack volume can be controlled in the Movie window transport controls.

To change the audio output destination of the movie soundtrack, open the Sequence Editor window and use the Track Selector to display the movie track. On the left edge of the movie track, there is a pop-up menu that allows the audio output of the movie to be sent to any pair of outputs on the audio interface or to an internal bus. If the movie audio is routed to a bus, that bus can then be routed to the input of an audio track or aux track for recording and processing.

It's also possible to extract the soundtrack from a movie into an audio track of the sequence. From the Movie window minimenu, select Add Track With Movie Audio.

Movie Offset Time

A movie is referenced to a SMPTE frame location in the sequence timeline. By default a new Digital Performer sequence starts at SMPTE frame time 0:00:00:00. In some cases, a movie will be referenced to a different SMPTE start time. Set the SMPTE start time of the movie in the Movie window minimenu.

It is possible to offset the start of the sequence in relation to SMPTE frame time. This allows the sequence to start in a location other than the beginning of the movie. To set the sequence start in relation to SMPTE, first locate the movie to where the sequence is intended to start. Note the SMPTE time in the counter in the Control Panel window. Under the right-hand counter, look for the name of the currently play-enabled sequence. Next to that is an Arrow button that opens a menu. The menu includes the option to Set Chunk Start Time.

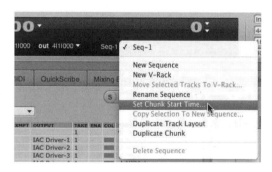

Figure 8.1

Choose that option, and the Chunk Start Time window will open. Change the SMPTE start time to the current location in the movie. Now the SMPTE time is referenced to bar 1 of the sequence timeline.

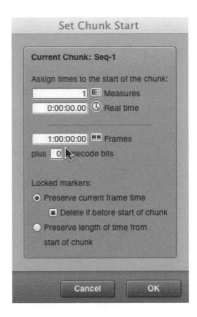

Figure 8.2

The sequence start time can also be programmed from within the Chunks window. Select the sequence chunk in the Chunks window and choose Set Chunk Start from the Chunks window minimenu.

Working with Multiple Sequence Chunks

If there are multiple sequence chunks in the Digital Performer session, the same movie will be used for each of the sequence chunks. It is possible for each sequence chunk to have a different timeline offset of the same movie. This allows a composer to work independently on separate musical cues that reference different locations in the movie.

It is also possible for each sequence chunk in a session file to reference a different movie file. To do that, open the first movie in a play-enabled sequence. One of the options in the Movie window minimenu is Use Same Movie For All Sequences. Check or uncheck this option as required.

Exporting a Movie with Bounced Audio

Once the new movie soundtrack has been created in the sequence, it is possible to create a new movie file that includes the new audio mix from the sequence. This is done as a bounce-to-disk operation.

Select a region in the Tracks window or the Sequence Editor window. If the selection is made in the Sequence Editor window, the movie track must be visible.

From the File menu, choose Bounce To Disk. In the Bounce window, click on the File Format pop-up menu and choose Quick Time Export: Movie. All other options in this window work the same way as bouncing audio only.

Click on the OK button. The next window will include options for creating a new movie. Select the desired options and click on the OK button. A new movie file will be created.

The audio from the selected region will be bounced into the soundtrack of the new movie. The original soundtrack for the movie will be replaced by the newly bounced audio. Therefore, if the original movie contained audio that needs to be part of the new soundtrack, the audio should be extracted from the original movie into a sequence track so that it will be included in the bounce.

Chapter 9

Exporting Media and Files

This chapter will discuss file output and CD burning from within Digital Performer. Digital Performer can export and generate different types of media files, including the following:

- Audio files
- MIDI files
- Movie files

Digital Performer can also be used to directly burn audio CDs. In addition, Digital Performer can generate files that are used to export content to other software programs. The raw audio files generated by Digital Performer are standard format files. It can also generate OMF, AAF, and XML files for sophisticated export of session data, as well as graphics files that can be printed to PDF format.

Bounce to Disk

It is possible to build up a complex session in Digital Performer with multiple audio tracks, virtual instruments, automation, and effects. The final step of the audio production is to create a single file that is the sum total of the mix. The final output of the mix can be mono, stereo, or multichannel for surround sound. Digital Performer can create an audio file on the hard drive. Digital Performer can burn audio CDs. If there is a movie included in the sequence, Digital Performer can create movie files.

Digital Performer creates the final output file with a process called Bounce to Disk. Bounce to Disk is essentially an automated process that records the output of the mix to a new file.

Bounce to Disk is a region-based operation. What gets selected is what will be included in the final bounced file. Make the selection of the tracks to be included in the bounce in the Tracks window or Sequence Editor window. If there are live virtual instruments in the mix, make sure that both the instrument tracks and the MIDI tracks are included in the selection.

Once the selection is made, choose Bounce to Disk from the File menu. The Bounce to Disk window will open.

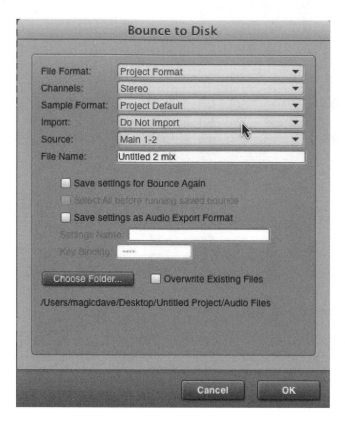

Figure 9.1

Bounce to an Audio File

- Digital Performer can create many different types of audio files. The most common formats are WAV, AIFF, and MP3. To select the type of file that will be created with the bounce, click on the File Format pop-up menu.
- Bounce to Disk will record a signal from the output that is selected in the Source pop-up menu. If the output of the mix is Built-In 1–2 for example, that's what needs to be set as the source in the Bounce to Disk window.
- The Bounce to Disk window provides options for File Format and for Sample Format. The File Format pop-up specifies the type. In general, leave Sample Format set to Project Default.
- The number of channels can be set for the final output of the mix. If the mix is stereo, choose either Stereo or Same As Source.
- The bounced file can be imported back into a new track in the sequence. It can be imported into the Soundbites window, but not a track. The bounced file can be created on the hard drive but not imported into the session file at all.
- The bounce file can be named, and its save location can be specified. By default, the save location of the bounce file is the Audio Files folder in the project folder.
- Once the options are set in the Bounce to Disk window, pressing the OK button will cause Digital Performer to make the bounce file. This process is faster than real time. That means that if the bounce selection is three minutes, it will take less than three minutes for Digital Performer to create the bounce file.

In addition to creating final mixes, the bounce function can also be useful for consolidating multiple tracks within a mix. For example, there could be six background vocal tracks with edits, automation, and plug-ins. Just those tracks could be selected and bounced to disk. The bounce file could be imported to a new track in the sequence. The original tracks could then be deleted or disabled and hidden in a track folder. This would provide a single stereo track with a printed mix of the background vocals.

Movie

Digital Performer can bounce to a movie file. If there is a movie in the sequence, that movie can be included in the bounce selection, and bounced to a new movie file. If there is any audio in the original movie file, that audio will be replaced by the audio from the Digital Performer sequence.

If the bounce selection does not include the entire original movie, the new movie will include only the selected video. If the bounce selection extends earlier or later than the original movie, Digital Performer will insert video black at the beginning or end of the new movie as needed.

CD

Digital Performer can bounce audio directly to a CD. In order to bounce to a CD, the sample rate of the session must be 44.1 kHz, and the sample format in the bounce window must be set to 16-bit Integer. That's because a commercial audio CD is formatted with 44.1/16-bit audio.

If the bounce selection is a single piece of music, that's what will be burned to the audio CD. In order to burn multiple songs to a CD, first bounce the individual sequences to stereo audio files. The stereo files can then be placed in a new sequence. The new sequence can then be selected and bounced to an audio CD, and the CD will include all the stereo audio files in the bounce selection.

When bouncing to a CD that will have multiple index points, index points can be based on soundbites, markers, or both.

Freeze Selected Tracks

Digital Performer can create new audio tracks based on existing audio tracks. Select one or more audio tracks and choose Freeze Selected Tracks from the Audio menu. Digital Performer will create a new audio track for each selected track.

Freeze Selected Tracks is a region-based function. The Freeze function will play back the selected region and record that signal into the newly created track.

Audio Tracks

The new audio track will now contain audio that is the playback of the previously selected track. The audio in the new track will be printed to include all automation, plug-ins, and edits from the original track. The new sound file is added to the Audio Files folder in the project folder. This makes it easy to find the new file if the contents of the Audio Files folder are viewed by date. The soundbites and sound files from the original track are still on the hard drive and referenced in the Soundbites window.

One use for freezing audio tracks is to conserve CPU power. If there are many plug-ins running on an audio track, freezing the track will create audio with those effects printed. The original track can then be deleted or disabled to conserve CPU power. Disable the ENA button for the original track in the Tracks window. This stops the track from using any CPU or disk resources while keeping it available in case it needs to be reenabled and changed at any time.

Virtual Instruments

Freeze Selected Tracks can be used to generate an audio file based on the output of a virtual instrument. Select the instrument track and any MIDI tracks that are triggering the virtual instrument. The region that is selected is what will be printed. Choose Freeze Selected Tracks from the Audio menu. This function is described in additional detail in chapter 6, "Virtual Instruments."

Exporting Audio and MIDI

In addition to playing back a sequence, Digital Performer can also create audio and MIDI files. These files can be exported in a variety of formats.

Audio Files

Soundbites can be exported from Digital Performer to create new sound files. This is a two-step process. The soundbite or soundbites must first be selected. The Export option is then available either from the minimenu of the Soundbites window or from the File menu.

The Export Soundbites window provides options to rename the new sound file, as well as choose the location to create the new file and the file type.

If multiple soundbites are selected and exported, each selected soundbite will result in a new sound file.

MIDI Files

Digital Performer will export MIDI tracks in Standard MIDI File format. Standard MIDI File is a type of file that can be opened by most MIDI sequencing software on Mac and Windows computers. Standard MIDI File format includes the contents of selected MIDI tracks and any selected tempo data in the conductor track.

Select the MIDI tracks to be exported. This is a region-based operation, so the time range of what is selected is what will be exported. MIDI tracks must also be play-enabled to be included in the exported MIDI file.

From the File menu, choose Export > Selection As MIDI File... A window will open that allows the Standard MIDI File to be named, and for its location to be specified.

Printing and Text Export

To print the contents of a Digital Performer window, choose Print Window from the File menu. The Print window also includes the option to print to a PDF file. It is possible to extract text from a PDF file.

Chapter 10
BUILD A SONG FROM SCRATCH

This chapter will describe step by step how to build a basic MIDI and audio composition. These steps are also described in the movies that are on the DVD that accompanies this book.

Launch Digital Performer and Create a New File

- Double-click on the Digital Performer icon to launch the software.
- On the Mac, press the New button. On Windows, press Cancel, then choose New > New from the File menu.
- Name the new file and choose a save location.
- Press Save. The new project will be created and Digital Performer will open to display a factory default new file template.

Check Audio and MIDI Input

- Go to Setup > Configure Audio System > Configure Hardware Driver.
- If an external audio interface is connected to the computer, select that interface.
- For virtual instrument triggering and monitoring audio through plug-ins, choose 128 or 64 for the buffer size. Click on OK to close the window.

Enable Click

- Double-click on the Click button in the Control Panel to open the Click Preferences window.
- Check that the Audio Click pop-up menu is assigned to the monitor outputs of the external audio interface or built-in audio outputs. If the output is displayed in italics, then that means it must be reassigned.
- Select click sounds for Accented and Normal from the pop-up menus. If a click sound appears in italics, it must be reassigned.
- If the Audition button is checked, a click sound should now be heard from the audio monitor outputs.
- Press the Done button to close the Click Preferences window.

- Press the Click button in the Control Panel to enable the click.
- When the Record or Play buttons are pressed, the click will play back through the audio monitor output.

Set Tempo

Drag the Tempo slider in the Control Panel window to set the initial tempo for the composition.

Create a MIDI Drum Track

- Go to the Project menu and select Add Track > Instruments With Options... An Add Instrument Track window will open.
- From the pop-up menu, select Sampler > Model 12.
- Click on the OK button. The Model 12 window will open. Also, an instrument track and record-enabled MIDI track will be created in the sequence.
- Choose a kit preset from the pop-up menu in the upper left-hand corner of the Model 12 window.
- Playing on an external MIDI controller will now trigger sounds within Model 12.
- Press the Record button in the Control Panel window.
- Play on the external MIDI controller to record a MIDI drum pattern.

Name Tracks

- Option-click on a track name to open a naming field.
- Type in the new track name.
- Press Return to exit the naming mode.

Set Up a Record Loop

- Press the Memory Cycle button in the Control Panel window.
- Set loop start and stop times by dragging the Repeat icons in the Tracks window, or by setting start and stop times under the counter in the Control Panel.
- Press the Overdub button in the Control Panel window.

Create and Record Virtual Instrument Tracks

- Go to the Project menu and select Add Track > Instruments With Options... An Add Instrument Track window will open.
- From the pop-up menu, select any listed virtual instrument.
- Click on the OK button. The instrument window will open. Also, an instrument track and record-enabled MIDI track will be created in the sequence.
- Choose a patch or load a sampled instrument, depending on how the selected virtual instrument works.
- Playing on an external MIDI controller will now trigger sounds within the virtual instrument.
- Press the Record button in the Control Panel window to record into the MIDI track.

Create and Record Audio Tracks

- The factory default new file template provides four mono audio tracks and two stereo audio tracks.
- To create additional audio tracks, go to Project > Add Track. Select a mono or stereo audio track. A new track will be added to the sequence.
- Name the audio track.
- Click on the input field for a mono or stereo audio track and select the input that corresponds with the incoming audio signal.

- If an input assignment appears in italics, it must be reassigned.
- Check the output field for the audio track. Make sure that it is assigned to the audio monitor output.
- If an output assignment appears in italics, it must be reassigned.
- Press the Rec button for the audio track to record-arm.
- Go to the Studio menu and open the Audio Monitor window.
- The record-armed input will be highlighted in the Audio Monitor window.
- Generate an audio signal into the selected input. The highlighted input in the Audio Monitor window will show VU activity.
- Adjust the level of the input signal to get a good record level in the Audio Monitor window.
- Go to Studio > Audio Patch Thru. Make sure that Auto is checked.
- The live input signal will now be audible at the audio monitor outputs.
- Press Record in the Control Panel to record audio into the track.

Set Up a Basic Mix

- Click on the Mixing Board tab to open the Mixing Board window.
- Go to the Studio menu and open the Track Selector window.
- Use the Track Selector to show or hide tracks in the Mixing Board window.
- Use the volume faders and pan controls to adjust track levels.
- Click on the Inserts for tracks to add effects plug-ins.
- To automate any mix parameter, enable Automation Record for the track, and change the desired parameter as the sequence plays.

Master and Bounce To Disk

- Go to Project > Add Track > Master Fader Track. A master fader will be added to the sequence.
- Add an MW Limiter plug-in to an insert on the master fader.
- Choose a mastering preset from the pop-up menu in the upper left-hand corner of the MW Limiter plug-in.
- Play the sequence and check the levels in the MW Limiter.
- If the mix is too loud and causing the limiter to drastically reduce gain, adjust the input level.
- If the mix is not loud enough for full level output, adjust the Threshold control to raise the mix gain.
- Once the mix sounds good and has proper level, select all tracks from beginning to end in the Sequence.
- Go to File > Bounce To Disk.
- Select the desired bounce file format.
- Check the destination of the bounced file.
- Check the name for the bounced file.
- Press OK. Digital Performer will create final bounced audio file.

APPENDIX: ABOUT THE DVD

The Demo File

On the DVD is a folder called Demo Project. Copy this folder to the hard drive connected to your computer. Open the Demo session file in Digital Performer.

- The demo file includes audio tracks, MIDI tracks, virtual instruments, subgroups, effects sends and returns, and a master fader. The purpose of the demo file is to show off a completed composition within Digital Performer.
- The original recorded tracks contain multitracked acoustic drums and an acoustic guitar with a built-in piezo pickup. The drums and guitar were played as an improvisational jam with no click track reference. Drums were played by Paul Wilson.
- Once the basic tracks were recorded, the Adjust Beats function was used to drag bar lines to musical downbeats for the purpose of creating a tempo map in the Conductor track. No tempo changes were made to the audio, but the tempo map provides accurate bar lines and bar numbering within the composition.
- MIDI tracks were then created to trigger virtual instruments. The MIDI tracks were used to trigger instruments within the MOTU MachFive 3 virtual instrument sampler. The MachFive 3 instruments were then printed into the sequence as audio tracks. Initially, the MachFive 3 audio tracks are muted. The MIDI tracks have been reassigned to the virtual instruments that ship with Digital Performer. This allows the reader to experiment with different sounds for those MIDI tracks. It is also possible to disable the MIDI tracks and enable the MachFive 3 audio tracks.
- The drum tracks are routed through a bus and aux track for a subgroup. There is a reverb send and return, and a master fader. There are effects plug-ins used throughout the mix.

Videos

The first seven videos show step-by-step how to create a finished composition in Digital Performer. There is a great deal of detailed information along the way about general operation of the software. The videos cover audio and MIDI recording and editing, effects, virtual instruments, and mixing and mastering to a final stereo audio file.

The eighth video shows how pitch automation works within Digital Performer. A vocal track is used to demonstrate pitch correction and rewriting the melody.

1. Launch Digital Performer and Create a New File
Running time: 5:28

This video shows how to launch Digital Performer and how to create a new file based on the factory default new file template. Once the file is open, do the following:

- Configure the audio interface. This includes setting the audio hardware driver buffer size for virtual instrument and live patch-through monitoring.
- Test the MIDI input in preparation for creating a new composition.

2. Click Track and MIDI Drum Pattern

Running time: 10:24

This video shows how to do the following:

- Set up an audio click
- Adjust the tempo of the sequence
- Create a drum pattern using the Model 12 drum virtual instrument
- Open and use the Drum Editor window, including the Paintbrush tool
- Add a beat-timed stereo delay to the Model 12 output
- Create a separate send and return to facilitate routing the snare drum through a reverb

3. Virtual Instruments and MIDI Editing

Running time: 9:06

This video shows you how to do the following:

- Create MIDI and virtual instrument tracks
- Record a bass and keyboard part
- Quantize MIDI
- Edit MIDI in the Sequence Editor window, MIDI Editor window and QuickScribe window
- Print the output of virtual instruments to audio tracks

4. Audio Recording, Editing, and Effects

Running time: 11:33

This video shows you how to do the following:

- Set up an audio input and record into an audio track in Digital Performer
- Edit audio, including cutting, copying, moving, and trimming
- Time-stretch audio
- Insert plug-ins, including the Tuner, Masterworks Leveler, and ProVerb

5. POLAR

Running time: 7:52

- Part 1 describes how to set up an audio signal to be monitored and recorded through effects plug-ins.
- Part 2 describes POLAR in detail.
- Rhythm guitar and lead guitar parts are recorded in POLAR.
- Takes are then exported to audio tracks in Digital Performer.

6. Track Comping

Running time: 7:28

- The lead guitar parts recorded in POLAR are comped to create a single master track.
- The master comp track is edited.
- Crossfades are added to the edits.

7. Mixing and Mastering

Running time: 10:18

- The final combinaiton of audio tracks and virtual instruments is balanced and mixed.
- Effects sends and returns are created.
- Subgroups are created.
- A master fader is created and a mastering limiter is placed on the master fader.
- The last step is to bounce the mix to disk and to make a stereo audio file.

8. Pitch Automation

Running time: 4:19

This video describes the following:

- Pitch-automation functions in Digital Performer
- Changing the melody of a vocal part
- Printing the changes to a new audio file

INDEX

quick PRO guides series

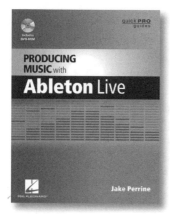

Producing Music with Ableton Live
by Jake Perrine
Softcover w/DVD-ROM •
978-1-4584-0036-9 • $16.99

Sound Design, Mixing, and Mastering with Ableton Live
by Jake Perrine
Softcover w/DVD-ROM •
978-1-4584-0037-6 • $16.99

The Power in Reason
by Andrew Eisele
Softcover w/DVD-ROM •
978-1-4584-0228-8 • $16.99

Sound Design and Mixing in Reason
by Andrew Eisele
Softcover w/DVD-ROM •
978-1-4584-0229-5 • $16.99

Mixing and Mastering with Pro Tools
by Glenn Lorbecki
Softcover w/DVD-ROM •
978-1-4584-0033-8 •$16.99

Tracking Instruments and Vocals with Pro Tools
by Glenn Lorbecki
Softcover w/DVD-ROM •
978-1-4584-0034-5 •$16.99

The Power in Logic Pro: Songwriting, Composing, Remixing, and Making Beats
by Dot Bustelo
Softcover w/DVD-ROM •
78-1-4584-1419-9 • $16.99

Logic Pro for Recording Engineers and Producers
by Dot Bustelo
Softcover w/DVD-ROM •
978-1-4584-1420-5 • $16.99

The Power in Cubase: Tracking Audio, MIDI, and Virtual Instruments
by Matthew Loel T. Hepworth
Softcover w/DVD-ROM • 978-1-4584-1366-6 • $16.99

Mixing and Mastering with Cubase
by Matthew Loel T. Hepworth
Softcover w/DVD-ROM • 978-1-4584-1367-3 • $16.99

HAL•LEONARD®

Prices, contents, and availability subject to change without notice.

0312